The Origins of Ludlow

The Origins of Ludlow

by
Dr David Lloyd

Logaston Press

LOGASTON PRESS
Little Logaston Woonton Almeley
Herefordshire HR3 6QH
logastonpress.co.uk

First published by Logaston Press 2008
Copyright © Dr David Lloyd 2008

ISBN 978 1904396 956

Typeset by Logaston Press
and printed in Great Britain by
Bell & Bain Ltd., Glasgow

This book is dedicated

with respect and affection

to the late Christopher Train, C.B.

Contents

Preface and Acknowledgements

This book seeks to summarise and evaluate all that has been written on the origins and early growth of Ludlow. Much in the book draws on the work of others, citing many authors – some of them scholars of repute, others less well known. In chapter 5, however, largely original work is presented, drawn from the study of Ludlow's plan and properties over the last thirty years. Finally, in chapter 6, a speculative model for Ludlow's origins and early growth is suggested as a stimulant for further debate and research.

It is fitting that this book has gone to our publishers in 2007, at the end of the academic year 2006-07, during which we have been celebrating the 30th anniversary of the Ludlow Historical Research Group. As asserted in an article in the Spring 2007 edition of *Local History News*, research by the group has 'transformed understanding of Ludlow's history', though many of our findings have yet to be published. We believe that this book is an important step in that process.

The contributions of those who have written and thought about Ludlow's origins and early growth is fully acknowledged in the text. The purpose here is rather to express my gratitude to the many people who have helped me to formulate my ideas on these subjects and to thank those who have played a part in the production of this book.

The content of the book has grown out of discussion with many people, among them members of the Ludlow Historical Research Group, people attending classes and lectures, visiting historians, and those reading papers at academic conferences. More specifically, I would like to thank the members of the *Historic Towns and Cities* lecture series, held at Ludlow Assembly Rooms in 2006-07. One session in that series was devoted to the *Origins and Early Growth of Ludlow* and provided an opportunity to present my case to a discerning audience. The response was enthusiastic, producing a lively discussion and several written submissions, some of which are referred to in the text.

I am greatly indebted to my colleagues on the Publications Sub-Committee of the Ludlow Historical Research Group – Jean Brown, Margaret Clark, Roy Payne, Chris Potter and the late Chris Train – all of whom read the text carefully and made constructive suggestions. I am grateful also to a number of distinguished scholars outside Ludlow who kindly agreed to read the text, and who made their expertise available to me: Sally Fielding (née Harvey), a notable Domesday scholar; Ron Shoesmith, Hereford and Welsh border archaeologist; and Terry Slater, of the University of Birmingham, a historical geographer with a long-standing interest in urban origins and development. Another reader was my school friend, Michael Faraday, who refrained from detailed discussion of Ludlow's origins in his *Ludlow 1085-1660: A Social, Economic and Political History*, published in 1991, referring generously to 'Mr D.J. Lloyd's forthcoming book'. I apologise to Michael and to others for the long delay.

Three people have made particular contributions. Ric Tyler, an architectural draughtsman now working for the Archaeology Unit of the University of Birmingham, has drawn the maps from my originals with great professional skill. Joanne Lindsay has read the text with care, correcting a number of errors and enhancing the content in several ways, often challenging me to defend my ideas. But my greatest acknowledgement is due to Christopher Train, who sadly died a few months before the book went to press.

Over the last ten years Chris and I had many discussions about the origins of Ludlow, some of them whilst Chris was preparing his own *The Walls and Gates of Ludlow*, published in 1999. His keen intellect and logical thinking did much to formulate my ideas and conclusions and have greatly benefited this publication. I am proud to dedicate this book to his memory.

Introduction

by Professor Peter Borsay,
Aberystwyth University

In 1955 the pioneering local and landscape historian W.G. Hoskins issued a heartfelt plea in his now celebrated *Making of the English Landscape*: 'There are, of course, many scholarly books on boroughs in their institutional aspects, their political history and their administration. But one looks in vain for any discussion of their physical growth, where their original core lay, of the directions in which they grew, and when, and why, and of what accounts for their street plan and shape to-day.' Fifty years on, how things have changed. No serious urban historian can now afford to ignore the townscape. David Lloyd's investigation – and it is a genuine detective story, with false clues and reports of human remains – of the origins and early history of Ludlow, illustrates triumphantly how far the lessons of Hoskins have been learnt.

The early chapters summarise the plethora of previous theories on the subject and examine the pre-Norman history of the site. However, it is in chapters 4 and 5 that the author gets to the 'meat' of his study, reviewing the documentary evidence, and – particularly in chapter 5 – rising to the Hoskins challenge: 'The English landscape itself, to those who know how to read it aright, is the richest historical record we possess.' In a forensic analysis of the town's burgage plots and streets, based on the dedicated work of the Ludlow Historical Research Group (of which David Lloyd was a founder member), the town's beginnings are revealed with compelling logic.

Historians, for whom Ludlow has become a test case of urban origins, will welcome this scholarly analysis of the documentary and physical evidence of the town's early history, and new interpretation proposed. Inhabitants of Ludlow will be grateful that, in an age when the pursuit of roots has become a popular passion, they now have as accessible and lucid an account as can be constructed, given the present state of knowledge of the birth of their town.

Chapter 1

The search for 'urban roots'

Proud citizens of towns and cities are often, like genealogists, involved in what has been called 'a search for roots'.[1] In many cases recourse is made to well-worn legends. Peter Borsay, for example, in *The Image of Georgian Bath, 1700-2000*, cites the tradition that the city was founded in 863 BC by Bladud, King of the Britons and father of King Lear.[2] Sometimes a precise event can be invoked, as at Ayr, where the town historian wrote confidently that 'history begins in 1197, when a castle was built by order of William the Lion, King of Scotland'.[3] Zeal for such a date has sometimes led civic authorities astray, as at Barnstaple in Devon, where a pillar of granite is carved with the words 'Millenary Stone, 930-1930', an ascription that came from belief in a lost charter which historians now condemn as 'an impudent invention'.[4] Occasionally, however, towns do have the luxury of a precise date, for example the foundation of the borough of Stratford-on-Avon in a pre-existing parish in 1196 by John Coutances, Bishop of Worcester.[5]

Ludlow is one of many towns which have no foundation dates that can be celebrated in this way. It is a market town in south Shropshire, a few miles from the Welsh border, with a current population of about 10,000.[6] The town has long been cited as dating from the Norman period, a distinguished scholar of urban studies, Maurice Beresford, Professor of Economic History at the University of Leeds, describing it in 1967 as 'a classic example of Norman town plantation'.[7] This study does nothing to alter this description, though some weight is given to the suggestion, considered fully in chapter 5, that parts of the town may date from the late Anglo-Saxon period.[8] What it does seek to do is to examine in detail the various suggestions that have been made about the processes of the development of Ludlow, and to postulate a tentative model of growth.

Within the time-span of the history of towns in England and Wales, Ludlow has a middle position. Archaeologists and place name analysts have identified 21 Roman towns with 'sufficiently specialised functions to be considered urban', with another 54 'small towns'.[9] Most of these became the sites of later settlements, the nearest to Ludlow being Worcester, called Vertis by the Romans. After two centuries when there was almost certainly a decline in urban life, an Anglo-Saxon revival of towns started in the 7th century, with Hereford a well researched local example.[10] The Domesday Book survey of 1086 records about 70 'more important towns', including nearly all those that later became centres of county administration.[11] Many counties, however, had no other urban centres at this time, as was the case in Shropshire, where apart from Shrewsbury, well established as the county town, the only borough listed was the fledgling settlement at Quatt, later to become Bridgnorth.[12]

It will be argued below that Ludlow developed principally during the 12th century, though with earlier roots, and that by 1200 the town had reached its full medieval extent. Ludlow was thus part of a widespread process of urbanisation that occurred in the two centuries after the Norman conquest in 1066. In Shropshire, no fewer than 47 places additional to the two Domesday boroughs had market and fair charters during this period.[13] Many of these had other urban characteristics such as specialist economies and a measure of self-rule, and can properly be described as towns, though there were some failures, including, in the south of the county, Burford, Lydham and Stottesdon.[14] Ludlow, important for the marketing of wool and the manufacture of cloth, was an undoubted success, with an estimated population of about 1,725 by 1377, making it the second or third largest town in the county.[15]

The surge of towns reflected a developing economy, with more emphasis on craft manufactures and trade, which encouraged towns to develop at nodal points. The towns also absorbed the expanding rural population, with manorial lords allowing migration from over-burdened rural communities. Within these parameters, landowners had strong financial motives for promoting towns. They collected rents from the residents, many of whom were burgesses with freedoms and rights not available to most country dwellers, and also tolls from the markets and fines from the courts.[16] Some Shropshire towns, such as Newport, were royal foundations, whereas others, like Much Wenlock or Bishop's Castle, were instigated by religious houses or bishops.[17] The majority, however, including Ludlow, were seignorial plantations, founded by the baronial lords who enjoyed great power along the Welsh Marches.

Many of the less successful towns declined in size and status during the economic and demographic difficulties of the 14th century, so that by the Stuart period there were only about 15 clearly recognizable 'towns' in Shropshire.[18] Ludlow, the headquarters of the Council in the Marches of Wales in the 16th and 17th centuries, was one of the most enduring, and was a centre of regional administration as well as a market town and manufacturing centre. It continued to thrive in the 18th and early 19th centuries as a fashionable social resort and a centre for glove-making and other important local industries. By this time many ports, spas and coastal resorts had become significant urban centres, but it was the mushrooming of manufacturing and commercial towns that transformed the urban landscape. Ludlow, with a population that had risen to over 5,000 by 1831, continued to prosper in the 19th century, as was shown in the recent Ludlow Historical Research Group publication *Victorian Ludlow* (2004), and to expand further in the 20th century.[19] The extent of change, however, has not seriously compromised its character as an historic town, which has been widely eulogised by poets, travel writers and journalists, among them Lewis Braithwaite of the University of Birmingham, who called it 'for many people the perfect historic town'.[20]

The extent of the borough of Ludlow in 1884 is shown in Fig. 1. It will be argued in later chapters that the parish boundary, marked with a thick broken line, was unchanged since the late 12th century. Ludlow's Victorian suburbs, some of which can be seen on Fig. 1, were still largely in the parish of Stanton Lacy. Fig. 1 also shows that Whitcliffe Common, an important economic resource for Ludlow during the greater part of its history, was still divided between the parishes of Bromfield and Ludford. In 1884 Ludlow Castle remained in its own parish, that of St Mary Magdalene, where worship had taken place in the Middle Ages in the Norman chapel with a round nave, one of the best known buildings within the castle walls.[21]

The area of the borough, the same as that of the parish, was 172 acres.[22] It was bounded on three sides by the River Teme and its tributary, the Corve. The long eastern boundary was man-made, marked most clearly by what became Portcullis Lane in the north and Weeping Cross Lane in the south. Economically, the town was part of an integrated unit that reached beyond these boundaries into 'the liberties of Ludlow' where Ludlow

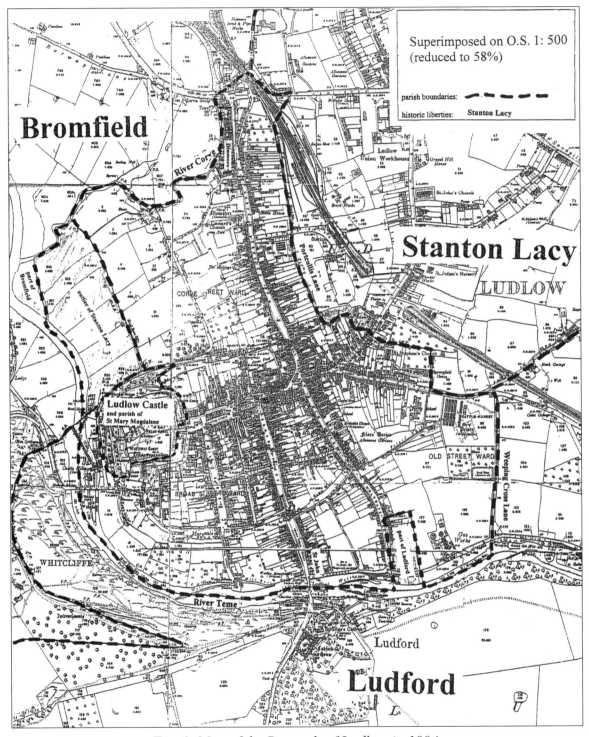

*Fig. 1. Map of the Borough of Ludlow in 1884,
showing boundaries and parts of adjoining parishes*

burgesses enjoyed rights and privileges. Within these liberties were a number of small closes and nine open fields cultivated by rotation, which brought the medieval town most of its food supply.

It is the purpose of this study to summarise and analyse the many books, articles, lectures and archaeological excavations which have considered the origins and early history of Ludlow. The archaeologist Hal Dalwood, who attempted an overview of this research in 1996, wrote that 'there have been more studies of the town plan of Ludlow than any other town in England', and asserted that 'a number of different hypotheses have been advanced for the development of the town'.[23] Dalwood's survey, however, though extremely useful, did not have access to all the sources of information available to the present writer, who believes that another synthesis is justified.

In chapter 2, previous work is reviewed. Some of this is documentary, where writers and scholars have used a range of sources, including genealogies, official papers and the writings of chroniclers and travellers. Over the last century the study and interpretation of maps has been of increasing importance, leading to the scholarly technique of plan analysis.

The nature of the site of Ludlow and the extent of early man-made features, which are described in chapter 3, together produce what has been called the pre-urban morphological frame – the disposition of natural elements and pre-Norman settlements and tracks that provide the influences and constraints on town plantation.

Chapters 4 and 5 provide the meat of this study. Chapter 4 concentrates on documentary sources, taking them in approximately chronological order, and establishing a small number of known dates which provide another kind of framework into which other material can be fitted, much of it inevitably speculative. A review of relevant archaeology is also included. In chapter 5 the plan units which have been identified are considered in turn, drawing on some of the findings already established, but making considerable use of map analysis, and also making comparisons with contemporary examples other than Ludlow itself.

The publication ends, in chapter 6, with a suggested model for the phased development of the Norman town, from a few years after the Conquest to the reign of King John, 1199-1216. With much published work available, some of it contradictory, with so many strands of different kinds of evidence, and with many great gaps in the record, it would be unwise to offer anything more positive. The hope is that what is presented here will stimulate further discussion and debate, and, most importantly, encourage more archaeological investigation.

Chapter 2

Published work from the sixteenth century on the origins of Ludlow, with an archaeological resumé

This chapter summarises the work of many of the authors, historians and geographers who have written about Ludlow's origins and early growth, taking them in approximate chronological sequence. Some analysis and assessment will be made, but in most cases this comes more naturally in later chapters. The chapter concludes with a brief review of relevant archaeological work.

William Camden

The first serious attempt to date the origins of Ludlow was by the Elizabethan scholar and antiquary, William Camden (1551-1623), who wrote of Ludlow in 1587, in his monumental work *Britannia*, that 'Roger de Montgomery first built a castle here which overlooks the Corve and from thence enclosed it with a wall'.[1] Camden, an assiduous compiler of information from earlier chronicles and oral traditions, clearly mistook the Corve for the more important Teme. By his reference to Roger de Montgomery, a henchman of William the Conqueror who held great estates on the Welsh border, Camden ascribed the castle to a date before 1094, the year when Roger died. Later scholars have convincingly shown that Roger Montgomery did not build any part of Ludlow Castle, but Camden's authority was such that the error persisted until it was corrected by the Shropshire historian R.W. Eyton. In his carefully researched *Antiquities of Shropshire,* published in 1857, Eyton argued that 'none other of the lords of the surrounding lands could have founded Ludlow Castle than Roger de Lacy'.[2] Camden's comments about the town wall again appear wildly inaccurate in view of the many documentary references indicating that this was built in the 13th century, but the reasoning by Christopher Train, in *The Walls and Gates of Ludlow* (1999), that the stone walls may have followed in part the line of earlier defences, gives renewed interest to Camden's account.[3]

Camden also described Ludlow as 'in Welsh Dinan', an interesting observation considered in more detail below as part of a wide-ranging review of Dinham, both as a location and as a place name. Camden called Ludlow *Lys-twysoc*, that is, *the Prince's Palace*, but this is probably a description of the state of the castle in the Tudor period, when it was indeed the seat of three Princes of Wales.[4] His descriptions are repeated by a number of later writers, but a variant came in 1785, when the scholar Thomas Wharton, an Oxford don, in compiling a new edition of the earlier poems of John Milton, included a description of Ludlow Castle, where Milton's masque *Comus* was first performed in 1634.[5] Wharton states that the castle was built 'about 1112', but no authority for this assertion has been found. As a possible oral tradition, however, it should not be dismissed entirely.

Thomas Wright

The publication of Thomas Wright's *The History of Ludlow and its Neighbourhood* in 1852 was another significant event for an understanding of Ludlow's origins. A less fastidious historian than Eyton, Wright (1810-77), who grew up in Ludlow, repeated Camden's error about Roger Montgomery,[6] but it was he who first popularised the enigmatic *Fitzwarine Romance*.[7] This is a prose tale in Anglo-Norman French, written in the early 14th century but based on a late 13th century verse romance which is now lost. It traces the fortunes of the Fitzwarine family of Whittington in north Shropshire from the Norman conquest to the early 13th century.[8] The first Foulke Fitzwarine comes as a squire to Ludlow Castle in the 1140s, when the countryside was beset with civil war between the two claimants to the English throne, Stephen and Matilda. Described as 'a weird mixture of accurate information, plausible stories that lack confirmation and magnificent flights of pure imagination', the accuracy of any part of the Romance is not easy to assess, though it has been claimed, perhaps rather generously, that the writer shows detailed knowledge of Ludlow and is 'at his best when writing about Ludlow castle'.[9] The Romance states boldly that 'the town which is now called Ludelowe was for a very long time called Dynan'. It also refers to 'a bridge of stone and lime' over the River Teme and to a castle with 'three baillies'.[10] The significance of these details will be considered below, as will the distinction made by Wright that the town of Ludlow, the *low* of which referred to a tumulus, 'continued distinct in name from the adjacent castle of Dinham'.[11] Wright's use of this and other place names was another innovative technique, taken further in more recent years by Margery Gelling and others.[12]

More knowledge of the region's 11th and 12th century history became available in the second half of the 19th century, as monastic chronicles were translated and published in the Rolls series and elsewhere.[13] From 1905, also, the Pipe Rolls Society volumes, over a 20 year period, revealed important details of the developing urban life of Ludlow from 1160 onwards, though no historian of Ludlow at that time, not even the highly regarded Henry Weyman, attempted a synthesis of the town's origin and early growth.

William St John Hope

A different approach was that of William St John Hope, a distinguished archaeologist who was for many years assistant secretary to the prestigious Society of Antiquaries. In 1903, with the permission of the owner, the Earl of Powis, St John Hope began a series of excavations at Ludlow Castle which led to the conclusion that parts of the inner bailey and the gatehouse were begun 'probably during the last quarter of the 11th century'. This endorsed Eyton's view that it was Roger de Lacy who started to build Ludlow Castle, beginning after he inherited the site in 1085. St John Hope added that 'on architectural grounds there can be no hesitation in believing that the castle was already built before Roger de Lacy fled the kingdom, after his second rebellion against the king, in 1095'.[14] St John Hope's findings were read to the Society of Antiquaries on 9 April 1908 and published in the 1909 volume of *Archaeologia*, the Society's scholarly journal. This is a seminal paper which forms the basis for all later research on the castle.

Whilst excavating at the castle St John Hope became interested in the origins and layout of the town, and on 6 May 1909 he read a second paper to the Society, called 'The Ancient Topography of the town of Ludlow, in the County of Salop'. This too was published in *Archaeologia* later that year.[15] His particular achievement was to interpret the topography or layout of the town as an indicator of its development, making use of plans published by the Ordnance Survey, which had surveyed Ludlow in 1884. He noted that the town was designed 'with great regularity into a number of more or less rectangular divisions',[16] concluding that: 'We are therefore confronted with the interesting feature of a town which was laid out not long after the Conquest and probably early in the 12th century'.[17] This was the first recognition

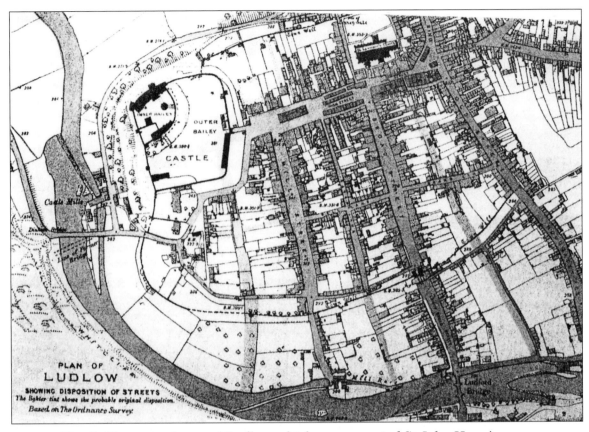

Fig. 2. The map of central Ludlow which accompanied St John Hope's paper on 'The Ancient Topography of the Town of Ludlow', published 1909

that Ludlow was a planned town, rather than one which had grown up haphazardly. St John Hope had other important insights into the process of later growth. The original High Street, he argued, had once been 'a broad thoroughfare' extending east and west along the high ground to the castle gatehouse, 'now represented by King Street, High Street, Castle Street and Castle Square', with an eastern end that had been 'considerably narrowed' and its western end 'encroached upon by later blocks of buildings'.[18] After describing the 'three other wide main thoroughfares' that ran southwards down the slope of the hill from the High Street, he also identified a number of redundant streets, including the 'curious strip of ground between Mill Street and Dinham'.[19]

Compared with later research, St John Hope's work had the severe limitation of confinement to the central and southern parts of the town, with Corve Street, Linney and Galdeford almost completely ignored. As a new way of looking at towns by map analysis his

10

work was, however, far-reaching. In his paper on Ludlow Castle he made the further point that Ludlow had been created out of the original manor of Stanton, which had been in the possession of Roger de Lacy in 1086.[20] After 1909 Ludlow was often cited as a planned town, e.g. by Butler, who, in a CBA report in 1976, described Ludlow, inaccurately, as 'one of only five towns in England laid out on a grid before 1140'.[21]

Beresford and Conzen: the gathering momentum in urban history

St John Hope was extensively quoted in Beresford's monumental *New Towns of the Middle Ages*, first published in 1967.[22] But whereas St John Hope had been primarily concerned with Ludlow's streets and their arrangement, Beresford gave great attention to burgage plots, the usually rectangular units of land held by settlers in return for an annual rent, which was often 12 pence, as at Ludlow.[23] Beresford introduced other technical terms into his description of Ludlow, referring to 'the chequer … almost a perfect rectangle' which was 'given to the church', while chapters on profits, site and chronology put what was happening at Ludlow into a wider context.[24] He also gave a reference to a Ludlow Corporation Burgage Rental of 1482, the beginning of the process of matching town plan and documents which has been undertaken by the Ludlow Historical Research Group from 1976.[25]

Almost contemporaneously, new methods and insights were being disseminated by M.R.G. Conzen, Professor of Geography at the University of Newcastle upon Tyne. Beginning his academic career in pre-war Germany, 'Con' Conzen, a refugee from the Nazis, did innovative work in historical geography at Newcastle in the years after 1945. His best known work was a detailed study of Alnwick, Northumberland, published in 1960, in which plan analysis and documentary sources are combined to show the development of what he called 'a composite townscape'.[26] Conzen carried out field work in a number of historic towns, including Ludlow, and in September 1966 presented a paper at an international conference of urban historians at Leicester University. Called 'The Use of Town Plans in the Study of Urban History', it used Ludlow as a prime example of Conzen's methodology.[27] The Leicester conference papers were published two years later in *The Study of Urban History*, edited by H.J. Dyos, then Professor of Urban History at the University of Leicester.[28] This work is generally regarded as a forerunner of the wave of urban studies which, over the next 35 years, transformed academic understanding of the history of towns and cities.

In his work on Alnwick, Conzen defined a town plan as 'the topographical arrangement of an urban built-up area in all its man-made features'. He recognized 'three distinct complexes of plan units: streets, blocks and buildings', an advance on St John Hope, who concentrated only on streets.[29] Conzen acknowledged that the plan is a palimpsest of a town's phases of growth and postulated that these are reflected in 'discrete plan units', each with its characteristic pattern of burgages.[30] In his 1966 paper, Conzen used Ludlow as an example of 'a composite medieval town', suggesting five 'distinct plan units.[31] The first of these was the castle, which he described as 'the pre-urban nucleus'. The second was 'the High Street plan unit', with its 'generously proportioned market place' and north-south burgages, occupying a characteristic *suburbium* position and including the original church. The third unit was the Bull Ring, Old Street and their east-west burgage series. The fourth, 'the southern plan unit', was the Broad Street-Mill Street unit, with its 'very regular layer of functionally differentiated streets'. Finally, there was the Dinham unit, which he found 'the most difficult to interpret', though he does make reference to 'the early village of Dinham'.[32]

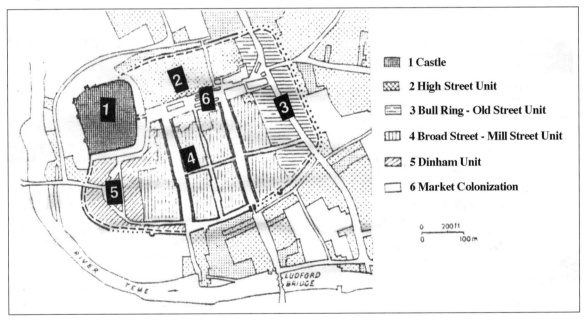

Fig. 3. Plan units from Conzen's 'The Use of Town Plans in the Study of Urban History'

The Ludlow Historical Research Group and its predecessors
At the time of Conzen's paper, local historians in Ludlow were beginning to study some of the Borough archives, by then held at the Shropshire County Record Office. A Workers'

Educational Association study group, with Frank Noble as tutor, transcribed and duplicated the burgage rental of 1619, though in the introductory notes the editor, E.L. Morley, commented that 'the absence of reference to the Palmers Guild is a mystery'.[33] Morley, a retired accountant, was the most active member, and began to compile notes on Dinham where he lived.[34] His belief that Dinham was 'the first borough' was cited by Beresford, but no supporting evidence was offered.[35] Morley's death and the commitments of Noble elsewhere put this work temporarily on hold. A short useful summary of what was then known of Ludlow's early history appeared in Trevor Rowley's *The Shropshire Landscape* (1972), with the salutary comment that 'the whole story is not yet fully understood'.[36]

The formation of the Ludlow Historical Research Group in 1976, led by Dr Martin Speight and the writer of this book, stimulated interest in many aspects of Ludlow's history, with a particular focus on properties. The distinction between freehold and leasehold soon became clear, the latter being Ludlow Borough Corporation properties, most of which had been inherited from the town's flourishing medieval Palmers' Guild. It was realised that the 1619 rental related to freehold properties only, but that there were other rentals for Corporation properties. Using leases, tax assessments and other records, these could be fitted together like jigsaw pieces to reconstruct streets. This break-through, which caused great excitement at the time, was the key to the system of tenurial reconstruction which was developed by the Group, as explained in its first publication, *Ludlow Houses and their Residents* (1977).[37] As will be shown below, this greater understanding of Ludlow's tenurial history had implications for the developing interest in the town's origins. One early finding was the prevalence of the perch measurement – 16 and a half feet – in Ludlow properties, many burgages having widths of two, three or four perches.[38]

Conzen (revised), Slater and others

Conzen's work continued to have great influence throughout the 1970s and 1980s and was cited in several publications, such as Colin Platt's *The English Medieval Town* (1976).[39] Conzen showed particular interest in Ludlow, taking a summer holiday cottage in Dinham for several years, when he had productive discussions with Ludlow Historical Research Group members. Conzen's published work was acknowledged as perceptive and stimulating, but an obvious limitation was his failure, like that of St John Hope, to include Corve Street, Galdeford and Linney. Though his 1966 paper implied a sequence of development, with the

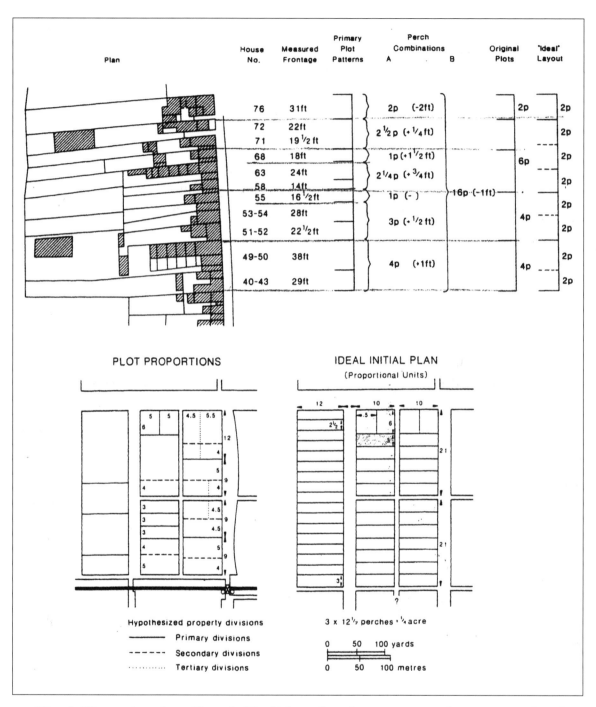

Fig. 4. Illustrations from Slater's 'English medieval new towns with composite plans'
Above: Metrological analysis of Lower Broad Street, Ludlow
Below: Geometrical analysis of Broad Street-Mill Street plan-unit, Ludlow

southern plan unit as the final phase, this had not been articulated. One attempt to rectify this was by Brian Hindle of the University of Salford, but little evidence was given to support boldly confident statements such as the attribution of 'the planned streets of Broad Street and Mill Street' to '1220-1260'.[40] In 1988 Conzen, now in retirement, produced a second paper, in which he too attempted to place his plan units in sequence, beginning with Dinham, where he saw the irregular layout of roads 'about the junction of Dinham and Camp Lane' as the remnants of a 'pre-urban village'.[41] One great insight from this paper is the suggestion that the High Street tract and the developments along Old Street, Bull Ring and Corve Street had common characteristics, with the 'deep burgages' found in both units providing 'a period index'.[42] This is in contrast to what he now called 'the Broad Street-Mill Street unit' with its generally shorter burgages and sophisticated street patterns.[43]

Significant work was done on Ludlow's plan, and also on the town's origins, by Dr Terry Slater of the University of Birmingham. Like Conzen, a historical geographer, Slater brought undergraduates to Ludlow to measure plot sizes. He has not attempted a complete analysis of the Ludlow plan, but used parts of it to illustrate general facets of urban development. In a paper published in 1981 he cited the west side of Lower Broad Street to show how *metrological analysis* – ground measurements followed by computation – reveals *blocks* of properties conforming to perch measurements, which were 'subdivided by the first landowners into smaller units'.[44] In a later paper, in 1990, in a collection of essays for 'M.R.G. Conzen on his eightieth birthday', Slater illustrated the more refined technique of *geometrical analysis* from the Broad Street-Mill Street unit inside the town wall, where three kinds of plots with different length-breadth ratios are identified, many of which were later divided into smaller holdings.[45]

In his 1990 paper, Slater also made several revisions to the Conzenian sequence of events. In particular, he thought it likely that Conzen 'has given too much prominence to the castle as the pre-urban nucleus'.[46] The long distance north-south route followed by Corve Street and Old Street is, he suggested, 'of equal importance', being 'the focus for the first elements of the town of Ludlow ... along the length of Old Street', while Dinham was 'developing at the same time ... to house the people more concerned with servicing the castle'. Some of Slater's ideas were given a wide currency by Hindle, who used Ludlow as a case study for his *Medieval Town Plans* in the *Shire Archaeology* series, also published in 1990.[47] His conjectural map of Ludlow *c*.1180 is shown on p.16.

Research on Ludlow Castle

Research on Ludlow Castle in the 1980s and 1990s also contributed to the debate about Ludlow's origins. Derek Renn, a Government actuary with a keen interest in castles, contributed a chapter called 'Chastle de Dynan: the first phases of Ludlow', to a volume of essays published in 1987 for D.J.C. King, a schoolmaster whose life-long scholarly interest in castles earned him the nickname 'King of the Castle'.[48] Renn argued that the entrance to the inner bailey faced south to what had been the original settlement at Dinham, and that the castle had been re-orientated when the outer bailey was added at a later date. 'The Dinham area', he pointed out, 'still has the air of a separate village with a late 12th-century chapel on the over-built village green facing the entrance to the first castle'.

Three other papers on the castle, by Bruce Coplestone-Crow, were published later, two of them in a collection of essays on *Ludlow Castle: Its History and Buildings* (2000). These reconsidered the dating of the first building of Ludlow Castle, suggesting that this occurred before 1086, and supplied newly researched information on some of the lords of Ludlow, with implications for the origins of the town.[49] These matters will be reviewed further in chapter 4. Another significant contribution was Train's book on *The Walls*

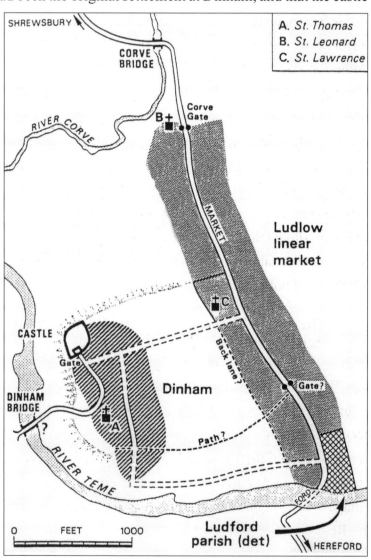

Fig. 5. Speculative map of Ludlow c.1180, from Hindle's Medieval Town Plans

16

and Gates of Ludlow, published by the Ludlow Historical Research Group in 1999. This established a chronology for the building of the town's defences, and had information and thoughts which are relevant to the wider issue of the town's origins.[50]

Place Names

In 1991 Margaret Gelling, Senior Lecturer at the University of Birmingham, after years of research with local volunteers, published her definitive work on *The Place Names of Shropshire*, and simultaneously made her extensive knowledge of street and district names available to members of The Ludlow Historical Research Group.[51] Discussion with Dr Gelling at this time also informed thinking on the place name Dinham. 'Din' can be taken to be the Welsh word 'hill', for much of the settlement is indeed on the side and top of a hill. 'Ham', is a common Anglo-Saxon word meaning 'settlement', so that the whole word can be interpreted as 'settlement on the hill'.[52] However, Gelling pointed out that all known occurrences before 1300 were 'Dynan' or 'Dinan', which seem to relate to Joce de Dinan, the Breton knight reputed to have come from Dinan in Brittany.[53] Various conundrums result. Joce de Dinan held the castle between 1140 and *c*.1150, so if 'Dynan' (Dinham) was named after him, should the settlement described above be dated from that time? Or did Joce take his name from a Ludlow settlement already called Dinan, as reported in the Fitzwarin Romance, which stated boldly:

> The castle of Dynan and all the land therebouts ... he gave to Sir Joce, his knight, who thenceforth took the name of Dynan and was always called Joce de Dinan.[54]

The genealogical details given would seem to rule out this scenario. Another explanation is that the area had a Welsh or Saxon name originally – possibly even Dinham itself – but became Dinan once Joce was its lord. The folk memory of that tenure lingered, so that three generations later the writer of the Romance, eager to magnify the importance of Joce, whom his hero Fulk Fitzwarine had served as squire, slightly over-emphasised his case that the village later called Dinham is contemporary with the castle. On balance, the evidence from the Romance is not enough to overcome the indications that the castle, and arguably the embryonic settlement at Dinham, date from the 1070s or 1080s.

The following year, 1991, saw the publication of Michael Faraday's meticulously researched *Ludlow, 1085-1660*: *A Social, Economic and Political History*. In his introduction

Faraday shelved 'the complex and fascinating subject of the planning and building of the town' for later publication by the writer of this book; but he had important points to make about place name evidence, concluding:

> It is likely, to judge by place-names and the lay-out of roads, that there were two or three earlier settlements, one of which may have been 'the first planned township of Dinham.[55]

Keith Lilley

As with Conzen in 1966, a paper with implications for the understanding of Ludlow's origins was presented at an academic conference in 1997. This was by Keith Lilley then of Royal Holloway College, the University of London. His paper on 'Colonialism and Urbanism in High Medieval Europe', presented at a conference on *Urbanism in Medieval Europe*, identified 'morphologies of urban change'. Within the tradition of 'plot patterns and street systems', as promoted by Conzen and Slater, Lilley named castle towns that were linked with the Norman conquest, citing Ludlow as an example.[56] Replicating two of Conzen's plan units, the castle and Dinham, Lilley described them as 'juxtaposed but morphologically distinct', concluding:

Fig. 6. The orthogonal plan of Ludlow, from Lilley's 'Urban Design before the Renaissance'

18

The likelihood exists that the two plan units were established at the same time, to complement each other, and the probable context for this is de Lacy's development of Ludlow castle…[57]

Later in his paper Lilley identified 'orthogonal plan-forms', in which the spread of geometrical thinking and understanding promoted sophisticated plan forms such as the Broad Street-Mill Street unit at Ludlow.[58] He suggested that this was laid out 'in the 1160s or 1170s', and cited contemporary features in parts of Coventry and at Drogheda in Ireland, another de Lacy town. A second paper by Lilley, in *Urban Morphology*, 1998, explores the resemblances between parts of Ludlow and Drogheda in greater detail.[59]

Review and Synthesis: early attempts

A number of attempts have been made to review some or all of this diverse evidence, though Lilley's important contributions, published in 1997 and 1998, have been overlooked. The Ludlow Historical Research Group held day conferences, in 1986 and 1999. The first, with Philip Barker of Birmingham University and Colin Platt of Southampton University among the speakers, focused especially on archaeology, with considerable discussion about Christ Croft, the ditch-like feature – perhaps a redundant street – between Mill Street and Dinham. The second included a powerfully argued paper by Train, which put the layout of the castle and Dinham within the context of other Welsh border towns.[60] He drew parallels with embryonic Norman towns established in the late 11th century, including Abergavenny in Monmouthshire and Longtown in south-west Herefordshire, the later a de Lacy borough. On Christ Croft, Train stressed that in all its early occurrences it was described as 'fossatum', the Latin word regularly used to describe 'a defensive ditch'. Another contribution at the 1999 conference was that by Dr Martin Speight, who suggested that the 'lud' of Ludlow may refer to the name of a Saxon chieftain, rather than to the loud waters of the River Teme, the interpretation offered by Gelling and others.

There have also been two written attempts to evaluate the different kinds of evidence. In 1996 Hal Dalwood, an archaeologist, produced an *Archaeological Assessment of Ludlow*. He gave a 'chronological outline' of the town's growth, and noted that there were 'a number of contradictory interpretations of the cartographic and historic data', citing St John Hope, Conzen, Slater and Hindle. 'At the moment' he affirmed, 'the various scenarios offered can only be tested against the internal logic of the analysis carried out', leading to the plea for

Fig. 7. A view of Christ Croft, shown diagonally in the centre of the aerial photograph, aligned top right to bottom left

the use of archaeological evidence.[61] A contributor to the assessment, Derek Hurst, listed the limited archaeological work that is available for interpretation. Excavations undertaken since 1996 can now be added to this list.[62]

The most recent overview of Ludlow's origins is a chapter by Ron Shoesmith in *Ludlow Castle*: *Its History and Buildings*, published in 2000. He reiterated earlier work by Houghton that the line of Old Street and Corve Street may have followed a Roman road, and stressed the importance of the 'large earthen mound' which was probably a tumulus on part of the site of St Laurence's parish church.[63] After weighing various options, he, like Slater and Hindle, favoured the view that the town had 'two separate parts'.[64] One of these was 'the Norman castle with its adjoining village of Dinham', but he accepted uncritically Hindle's view that the other was 'a thriving roadside settlement stretching from the river Teme … over Ludlow's hill to the river Corve'. A later development was the creation of 'the market area along the ridge', and then the laying out of Broad Street and Mill Street, 'two magnificent wide roads', with their appendages.[65] He concluded by reviewing the construction of the walls and gates, presenting a similar scenario to that suggested independently by Train, with parallel comparisons with other border towns.[66]

Archaeological Resumé

The first serious archaeological investigation in Ludlow was that in 1861, on the site of the Austin Friary in Lower Galdeford,[67] but the results, though valuable in other ways, add nothing to an understanding of the town's origins and early growth. St John Hope's excavations at the castle from 1903 to 1907, however, contributed greatly to knowledge of the castle, though the opportunity was lost to excavate in the outer bailey, where Hope himself postulated extensions of the High Street market place and the defensive ditch/redundant street, Christ Croft.[68]

The most significant excavation in the second half of the 20th century was on part of the site of the Carmelite Friary on the west side of Corve Street, towards the lower end. This was undertaken in the mid-1980s by Birmingham University Archaeological Unit, led by Annette Roe, working in collaboration with the Ludlow Historical Research Group. The results of the excavation, presented by Peter Klein and Annette Roe in *The Carmelite Friary, Corve Street, Ludlow: Its History and Excavation* (1987), were concerned primarily with the Friary itself, established in 1350, but the lowest level of excavation revealed, beneath the Carmelite refectory, shallow scoops containing fragments of domestic pottery; and also a line of postholes, interpreted as 'the back wall of a timber building fronting onto Corve Street.[69] Evidence of a larger building, possibly an aisled hall facing onto the street, was found at a higher level. These buildings, Klein and Roe concluded, 'span the greater part of the 12th and 13th centuries', an implication that the earliest building dates from before 1200, and was presumably the first building on the site after this part of the town had been burgaged, sometime before 1186.

In addition to those listed above, more than 60 identified archaeological sites and finds have been recorded by Dalwood and others (1996) on a base map of Ludlow, and more sites have been investigated during the last decade.[70] Most of these are post 1200 and shed little light on the town's origins. Some give information on buildings, including an excavation in 1973 which identified the floor of the nave of St Thomas's chapel, west of the standing structure.[71] This showed that the present road past the chapel must originally have been a short distance further west. Excavations at the rear of 10 King Street in 1983 revealed human bones, confirming the supposition that this edge of the street had encroached onto the churchyard.[72]

Some excavations relate to burgages. An excavation in 1975 by a Ludlow archaeologist, Michael Wise, established that the long burgages on the north side of Castle Street did reach to the town wall, with no evidence for termination nearer the street.[73] Marches Archaeology, in 1998, on the site of Nos. 82 to 91 Lower Galdeford, showed that the more western plots, as revealed by building foundations, were differently shaped from those to the east, perhaps reflecting the earlier form of open field strips.[74] The written report speculated that: 'It may imply that the eastern plots were laid down at a later date than those closer to the town to the west'. A contemporary trench sunk south of Friars' Walk confirmed the documentary evidence that this area was not burgaged. Excavation in 1999, by Gifford and Partners, on the Tesco site in Corve Street, confirmed at least one of the supposed burgage boundaries (F43B, along the south side of Station Drive), while animal bones found in one of the trenches were dated 'at about 1170', further evidence of early occupancy in Corve Street.[75] One of the most significant findings was that from the 1990 excavation in Lower Mill Street on the Ludlow College Sports Hall site, which found evidence of buildings along the line of an extension of Raven Lane, a classic case of archaeology confirming map analysis.[76]

There have been significant excavations relating to the town's defences. In 1990, 'some indication of a rock cut ditch' was found south-east of the outer curtain wall of the castle.[77] Marches Archaeology in 1998 showed that the ditch was approximately 7 metres (23 feet) wide and 2.5 metres (8 feet) deep, indicating that the defence here was formidable[78], but less so, for example, than at Montgomery, where the ditch was 36 feet wide at the top and 18 feet at the bottom.[79]

The most dramatic single discovery at Ludlow was that of a 7th-century dagger pommel, found in the summer of 1994 on the riverbed at an old ford at Dinham.[80] This has been assessed by British Museum specialists as 'of very high quality workmanship and great beauty', with 'analogous pieces usually coming from royal or aristocratic burials in Kent or East Anglia', but its implication for Ludlow is probably simply an indication of early use of the ford below Dinham.

Chapter 3

The site of Ludlow and its pre-Norman history

This chapter will describe the physical features of the site of Ludlow and will consider its early road systems – the morphological frame. It then reviews the evidence for the early development of the site, with particular attention to church history, beginning in the 6th century, when, according to medieval chroniclers, Irish saints were buried in an earlier mound or tumulus. Place name evidence is analysed and references to 'Luda the infidel' are also reviewed.

Physical features

Medieval Ludlow occupied the top and sides of a tilted block of land, projecting westwards from higher land to the east. To the west it is separated from the upland known as Whitcliffe by the gorge of the River Teme, through which the river flows to the south. The rapids over which the river once dropped, now masked by weirs, caused 'the loud waters' which, it has long been argued, gave the town the first part of its name, *lud*.[1] A tributary, the Corve, joins the Teme a short distance north of the town and the alluvial plain and gravel terraces of these rivers have been important physical influences on Linney and lower Corve Street.

The top of the tilted block provides a broad, almost level ridge at a height of about 350 feet above sea level. The prehistoric tumulus (*hlau*), traditionally alleged to have given the town the second part of its name, was situated on this ridge on the site later occupied by the parish church, as were the Norman castle and market place.[2] To the south the ground drops 100 feet to the River Teme over a distance of about a third of a mile, giving a gradient of 1 in 16. A high proportion of the houses of the medieval town were on this slope, with the streets climbing steadily up from the river to the market place. To the north, where the slope reflects a geological fault, the gradient for a short distance is in places 1 in 6, though in Linney it then drops almost imperceptibly to reach the Corve at just under 270 feet above sea level. Further east, Corve Street, the principal routeway out of the town to the north, takes a rather gentler slope of 1 in 12 as it drops down from the Bull Ring. Corve Street is the longest of the town's main residential streets, reaching half a mile to Corve Bridge.[3]

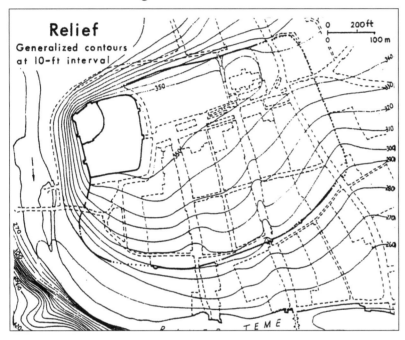

Fig. 8. Relief map of the walled town of Ludlow and extra-mural suburbs to the south[4]

East of the Bull Ring, Lower Galdeford falls obliquely across the contours towards the River Teme, but Upper Galdeford rises gradually to 380 feet above sea level at the top of Gravel Hill, a high-level river terrace of sand and gravels. In the Middle Ages this area was called 'the Sandeputtes', while Gravel Hill was 'the way to the Sandeputtes'.[5] From the backs of the properties on the east side of the lower part of Corve Street, the gradient is much steeper, up the slope now occupied by Hill Side and Quarry Gardens. Further east the land continues to rise, reaching 425 feet at Rock Green, at the extremity of the medieval liberties of Ludlow. To the west, the land behind Whitcliffe reaches heights of over 600 feet, but there is lower land north and south of the town, in the valleys of the Corve and Teme. The 16th-century poet Thomas Churchyard described Ludlow as standing 'most part upon an hill', but it is also a gap town, between the Welsh uplands to the west and the Clee Hills to the east.[6]

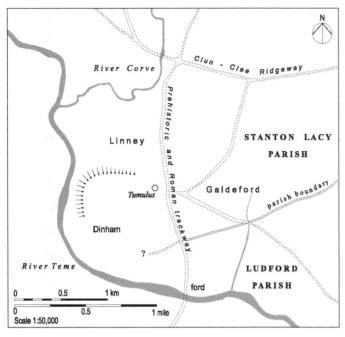

Fig. 9. Some elements of Ludlow's pre-urban landscape

The Morphological Frame

Conzen drew attention to the 'morphological frame' of pre-existing roads and tracks which were another influence on Ludlow's development.[7] He referred to the ancient north-south route-way along the line of Old Street and Corve Street and suggested that Upper and Lower Galdeford might also 'antedate the building up of the area'. This north-south route-way was used in prehistoric and Roman times and was certainly an important influence on the later town plan.[8] Another early track was the Clun-Clee ridgeway, first identified by Lillian Chitty, which intersected with the north-south route-way at what is now the bottom of Corve Street.[9] These early trackways, with other features, are marked on Fig. 9.

Two other roads, now called Lower and Upper Galdeford, converge at what is now Tower Street and the Bull Ring, but their original focus was almost certainly the tumulus which stood just west of the Bull Ring. This convergence suggests 'a long history of procession'[10] to the site, the purpose of which is considered below.

Alleged sixth century burial of Irish saints

Speculation about the early history of Ludlow emanates from the rebuilding of the church in 1199/1200, when medieval chroniclers report that the bodies of 6th-century saints were found on the site. The 19th-century historian Eyton dismissed this tradition as a fraudulent attempt to provide Ludlow with holy relics[11] – a well attested means of fundraising at that time – while Faraday suggests a possible connection with the de Lacys, 12th-century lords of Ludlow, who had strong Irish connections.[12] Nevertheless, there is some evidence to support the credibility of the claims of a 6th-century burial.

There are two accounts of the finds of 1199/1200, both probably altered versions of a single lost source. The fullest account is the *Collectanea* of John Leland (1506?-1552), the traveller and antiquary, who collected voluminous documents. This version is cited in Wright's *History of Ludlow*.[13] A shorter but perhaps earlier account comes from the *Llandaff Chronicle*, a diary of local and national events probably compiled by a monk of Wigmore Abbey.[14] Translations of the two accounts by Michael Faraday are given as Appendix 1.

Both versions describe stone coffins or tombs in which the relics were found, but there are differences about their location. Llandaff says the coffins were found in the foundations of a church when that church was rebuilt, but Leland locates them in 'a great mound of earth' – the tumulus – to the west of the church, where they were discovered when 'it was necessary to level the earth', so that the church could be 'extended'. Little is known about this pre-1199 church, but J.T. Irvine, the clerk of works for the 1859-61 restoration of St Laurence's, concluded from surviving fragments that it was 'of no mean description, consisting of a nave, a south aisle, perhaps some kind of transepts and a chancel'.[15] If the Leland account is accurate, the tumulus must have been at the western end of the present churchyard, perhaps adjoining College Street, whereas the early church was further east, perhaps towards the east end of the present nave.

The two accounts agree on the names of the Irish saints. All have now been identified as relatives of St Brendan (484-577), an energetic Irish missionary who travelled in Wales in the 4th century AD: his father Fercher, his mother Corona and his uncle Cachel.[16] Irish emigrants are known to have settled in parts of Wales in the 4th century AD, while 'the distinctive Irish style of Christianity was the dominant strain in Mercia in the mid 7th century'.[17] The feasibility of Brendan or his followers using an earlier tumulus at Ludlow as a Christian burial site in the 6th century cannot be discounted, though supporting evidence is lacking.

The accounts agree that the remains were revealed and re-interred – Leland cites a wooden vault – on 3 Ides of April (i.e. 11 April), but they differ by a year: Leland gives 1199, Llandaff 1200. Both accounts refer to a wooden plaque on which the names of the saints were inscribed 'in English', with lead on the outside and wax inside. The survival of such a memorial is doubted by Faraday and, it must be conceded, the description of it weakens the credibility of the narratives.[18]

Place name evidence, 1: *low* or *hlau*

On the other hand, place name evidence gives some support to the possibility of a 6th-century burial. The suffix *hlau-* or *low-*, which first appears as Lude*laue* in 1138, has traditionally been interpreted[19] as a prehistoric tumulus, presumably that on the present site of St Laurence's, described in Leland's manuscript to have been 'a great mound' that was levelled in 1199. It is tempting to associate the tumulus with the Bronze Age necropolis on the Old Field at Bromfield, two miles to the north-west of Ludlow.[20] This vast burial ground, on the felden area ('the Old Field') near the confluence of the Rivers Teme, Corve and Onny, seems to have been in continuous use for over 800 years from 1800 BC, and there is evidence of earlier Neolithic activity in the area.

The various meanings of *hlau* have attracted much scholarly attention. The word can mean simply 'hill', but Ekwall, a pioneer of place name studies, pointed out in 1936 that the meaning was often 'burial ground', especially when positioned after a personal name.[21] More recently Dr Della Hooke of the University of Birmingham, drawing largely on examples in Warwickshire and Worcestershire, has shown that *hlau* sites are often Bronze Age tumuli in which later Anglo-Saxon burials were inserted.[22] Examples cited where archaeological excavation has occurred have all yielded Saxon pagan, pre-Christian burials, but it is plausible that Christian burials also occurred, as may have been the case at Ludlow.

Place name evidence, 2: *lud*

The traditional interpretation of *lud*, the prefix of the name Ludlow, is as a topographical place name, referring to the rapids that were a feature of the River Teme as it dropped through Whitcliffe gorge on the west, south-west and south sides of the town.[23] The credibility of this view is increased by the fact that '*lud*' also occurs in the name Ludford, the parish facing Ludlow on the south side of the River Teme, with what seems to be a similar meaning – 'ford by the rapid'.[24]

As an alternative to the above view, it has been suggested that the *Lud* of Ludlow may be a reference to a tribal leader of that name.[25] Many urban foundation myths embrace a Lud, such as Ludeca, an early 9th century ruler of Mercia, or King Lud, a legendary 1st-century AD founder of London,[26] and this has promoted a general cynicism about the suggestion of Lud the tribal leader. However, a specific reference to *Luda the infidel* in the accounts of the finding of the Irish saints in 1199/1200 gives more credibility to the suggestion. It is stated in both Leland and Llandaff that the burial of the saint occurred '15 years after the death of the infidel Luda', suggesting that he might have been a 6th-century tribal leader whose name was perpetuated centuries later by the place name Ludlow.[27]

Ecclesiastical History during the Anglo-Saxon period

Much information is available about the ecclesiastical history of the area from the 6th to the 11th centuries. Some of this is relevant to speculation about what took place at the future site of Ludlow and to the likely date of the building of the pre-1199 church.

Ludlow now has a central position in the diocese of Hereford, an elongated wedge of land east of the central Welsh massif, stretching from the Severn in the north to beyond the Wye in the south. This was once the territory of the Magonsaetan, a Saxon people who from the 7th century occupied the western part of the then kingdom of Mercia – hence the name 'Westerners' by which they were sometimes known.[28] This, it has been said, was 'the last phase of the Anglian advance against the Britons of Wales', forcing the latter to retreat to their 'mountainous heartland'.[29] Further east, in the Severn valley, were the Hwicce, another Saxon people occupying most of Worcestershire and southern Warwickshire, while further north, stretching into what later became Staffordshire, were the south and north Mercians.[30]

In the early 7th century these territories were ruled by the formidable Penda, a pagan, but under his successors Christianity spread across the area.[31] Later in the century, probably before 680, separate dioceses were created, including that of Hereford.[32] The first known ruler of the Magonsaetan in that diocese is Mertewalh, a member of a royal Mercian family, who is said to have been converted to Christianity by a Northumbrian priest.[33] His large family included Milburga (d.722), who is reputed to have founded a nunnery at Much Wenlock, about 20 miles north east of Ludlow, and became its first Abbess. Other legends about St Milburga abound, including that relating to Stanton (Lacy), the parish out of which the new town of Ludlow was later created. One such legend describes how she was chased by a Welsh prince, from whom she escaped over the River Corve, which immediately turned into an impassable torrent, for which deliverance Milburga founded a church on the spot.[34] The story attests to Christian activity in the area as early as the late 7th century. A similar legend refers to Stoke St Milborough, a village a few miles north-east of Ludlow, which preserves the saint's name locally.

Minsters and Parishes

Attention has been drawn to the dominance of minster churches in the first centuries of Anglo-Saxon Christianity. These were centres of Christian mission, from which priests evangelised the surrounding countryside, often founding satellite churches. There were several minsters in the Ludlow region, including Leominster, 'one of the biggest mother parishes known in England', from which a remarkably large area was evangelised.[35] The parish church of Leominster still retains the proud title of minster, and serves a group of parishes taken from its former area of dependence. The cores of other former minster lands survive as large and irregularly shaped parishes in south Shropshire, as at Diddlebury and Stottesdon, with smaller parishes around them. Another minster in the immediate vicinity of Ludlow was Bromfield, described before the conquest as 'a wealthy minster of royal foundation', with a number of outlying possessions in the 12th century, including two small parishes, Halford and Ashford Bowdler. Ludford, facing Ludlow across the River Teme, was another parish with ecclesiastical links with Bromfield, and may once have been an outlying member. Stanton Lacy, on part of which the town of Ludlow was eventually built, was also a minster church. This was a large parish with a number of members, two of which, Hopton Cangeford and Cold Weston, later became independent parishes.[36] Some of these parishes are shown on Fig. 11.

The Anglo-Saxon period, it has been argued, was 'a melting pot of diverse and sometimes fiercely competing influences from British, English, Irish, Frankish and Roman sources', with the Danish wars a disrupting force in the 9th century.[37] Some degree of separation from the Celts further west, however, did occur in the later 8th century, when Offa's Dyke, a great linear bank and ditch, was built by order of Offa, King of Mercia, 757 to 796. To what extent the future site of Ludlow was affected by these processes is a matter of conjecture, but certainly there was considerable activity in the area. From about 950 this took the form of a weakening of minster organisation, and a greater role for individual parishes, many of them appropriated from former minster territories. 'Between 950 and about 1100', Blair has written, 'the building of thousands of small churches, mainly by manorial lords, transformed the ecclesiastical face of England'.[38] Several churches in the Ludlow area have architectural features dating from these years in the Saxon and early Norman styles, one of the best examples being Stanton Lacy itself, probably from the 'late 11th century'.[39] It has been suggested, however, that the dedication to St Peter and the presence of a Roman villa north of the church, may reflect 'more ancient foundations'.[40] The enigmatic font in St Laurence's parish church, which appears to have been hollowed from an upturned Roman column, is another pointer to early Christian activity on or near this site, and may date from the pre-1199 church, or even from a yet older building on the site.

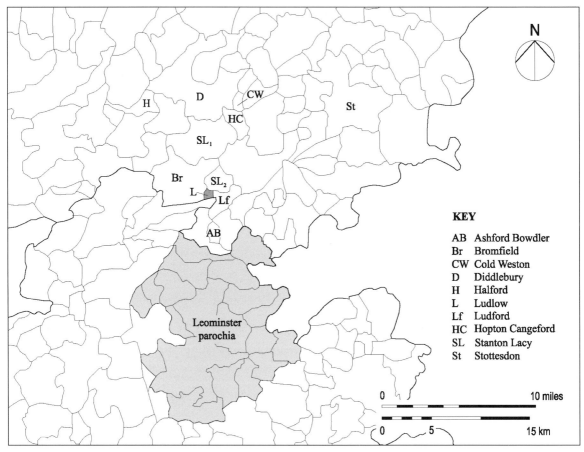

Fig. 10. Domesday Parishes of north Herefordshire and south Shropshire mentioned in the text (after Gelling, 1992)

Early history of the site of Ludlow

The site of medieval Ludlow was once part of the large Saxon parish of Stanton, now Stanton Lacy. The two manors – Stanton Lacy and Ludlow – often shared a common seigneurial history in the 12th and 13th centuries, when they belonged to the powerful de Lacy family. Until the 19th century, part of Linney remained an outlying portion of Stanton Lacy, showing that the site of the planned town had been taken from the rural manor.[41] This can be seen in Fig. 1.

It is also likely that the south-east part of medieval Ludlow once belonged to the adjoining parish of Ludford, parts of which were north of the River Teme. Part of the ancient boundary between Stanton Lacy and Ludford survives as Rock Lane, two parallel entrenched ditches with a narrow ridge between them.[42] Within the boundary of medieval Ludlow the line of Rock Lane continues as the lower part of Friars' Walk, the intervening section having been diverted following licence to the Austin Friars in 1284.[43] The boundary probably continued south-westwards to meet the River Teme, but the detached portion of Ludford parish which survived to the south as an administrative unit until the 19th century (see Fig. 1, p. 4) strengthens the view that part of the land for Ludlow was taken from that parish. Within the parish of Ludford the land that later became Ludlow was initially part of the barony of Castle Holdgate, held at the time of the Domesday Book survey in 1086 by Helgot, under Roger de Montgomery of Shrewsbury Castle.[44]

Until the 19th century rents from the lower part of Old Street were paid to the Lord of Holdgate, so that this part of the town was known as Holdgate Fee. This association with Roger de Montgomery may account for the mistaken but long held belief that he was the founder of Ludlow Castle.[45]

The place names Galdeford, Linney and Dinham, all referring to this day to districts rather than to single streets, are other place names which may have early origins. Faraday has suggested that Galdeford was a farmstead or even a township, perhaps centred at the bottom of Lower Galdeford, where a former stream, now culverted, was once crossed by a ford.[46] *Galde* may derive from the Old English *gelad*, meaning 'difficult river crossing'.[47] Linney, which now refers to the steep slope north of the town centre and to the low lying area beyond, is certainly an Anglo-Saxon place name, probably referring to 'the dry land (*ey*) above the flax growing area from which linen was produced.[48] The use of such a name suggests that there was economic activity in the area, and perhaps some habitation, just off the ancient north-south route-way. Dinham, the area south of the castle site, is the most problematic of these place names, but is most appropriately considered in chapter 4, after the documentary evidence has been reviewed.

Review of speculations made in this chapter
In spite of the doubts expressed by some historians, the chroniclers' accounts of the 6th-century burial of Irish saints in an older tumulus do have some credibility. The place name

evidence that *hlau* often refers to Anglo-Saxon burials in an older tumulus certainly gives some support to the plausibility of these burials, as do the indications of early Irish influence in Mercia. Equally, the chroniclers' references to 'Luda the infidel' give weight to the view that the *lud* of Ludlow is a personal rather than a topographical place name. Nevertheless, the authenticity of both the 6th-century burials and 'Luda the infidel' must remain open questions.

It has been shown that there was considerable Christian activity in the Ludlow area from the time of St Milburga, but none of this can be firmly tied to the site of St Laurence's. Irvine's description of the pre-1199 church is not precise enough for any deductions about its antiquity to be made, though the enigmatic font still in use at St Laurence's is perhaps suggestive of an early date. The convergence of tracks at the tumulus, still visible in the present street pattern, is another indication of the importance of the site, perhaps as a place of veneration.

The chapter concluded by reviewing the administrative history of the area in the Anglo-Saxon period, showing how the earlier minsters and the later parishes have left their imprint on the landscape, creating a template that guided later growth. Finally, there was further resource to place names to indicate possible pre-Domesday activities.

Individually, the literary, topographical and place name evidence is thin. Together, they strongly suggest that Ludlow was a place of occasional resort, if not of permanent habitation, well before the Norman plantation. While the place names suggest farming, they also confirm the other indications of a sacred site probably pre-dating Christianity, hallowed by pious legend and perhaps the tangible presence of an early Christian church.[49]

Chapter 4

Documentary sources of information, considered chronologically

This chapter focuses on the wide variety of sources which give information about the years of Ludlow's origins and early growth. Much of it concerns the Norman barons who successively held the lordship, especially members of the de Lacy family. At first documentary references to the town are few and not always reliable, but after 1154 there are more official records, reflecting in part the better administrative systems introduced by King Henry II.

Walter de Lacy I, first Norman Lord of Ludlow

Although much of the detailed planning must have been delegated, the influence of the lord over the foundation and growth of a seigneurial new town was paramount. An account of events at Ludlow after 1066 must begin, therefore, with the lordship. The sequence starts with William fitzOsbern, 'steward of Normandy and the Conqueror's closest confidant'.[1] After the Norman Conquest of England he was given great estates on the Welsh border, many of which were tenanted by Walter de Lacy I, apparently fitzOsbern's second in command. Together fitzOsbern and de Lacy fought the Welsh of Brycheiniog and Gwent. After fitzOsbern's death in 1071, and the unsuccessful rebellion against the king by fitzOsbern's son in 1075, the king granted many of the fitzOsbern lands to Walter de Lacy I, including 163 manors to hold in chief, making him one of the foremost barons in the Welsh Marches. Many of these lands had previously been held by the rich Englishman, Eadwig Cild, and

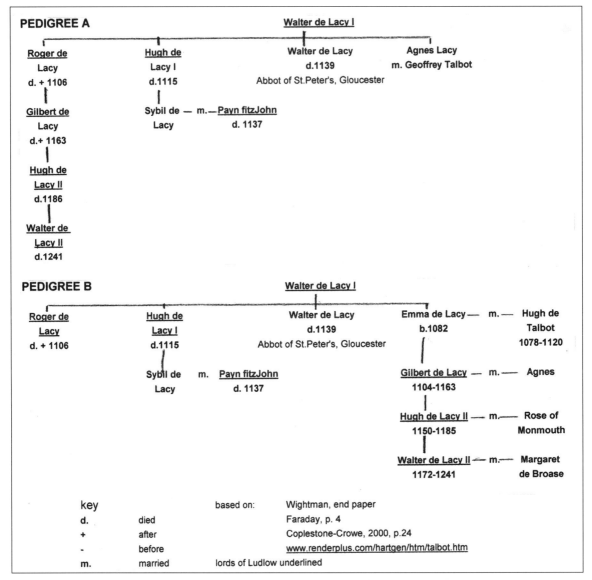

Fig 11. Alternative pedigrees of the de Lacy family

other lesser thanes. Wightman,[2] Faraday[3] and others have presented a generally accepted pedigree of the de Lacys (Fig.11A), but an alternative interpretation of the limited source material available is offered in this publication (Fig. 11B).[4]

Walter de Lacy came from Lassy in Normandy, just south of Falaise, where his name is on the list of knights who followed Duke William to England, prominently displayed in the Town Hall. The shape of the bailey of the castle of the de Lacys can be seen but the only surviving stones are reputedly incorporated in a 17th-century barn.[5] The greatest concentration of de Lacy lands in England was in Herefordshire, where Weobley, with an early motte and bailey castle, became the de Lacy caput or chief manor, as it had been for Eadwig Cild. There was, however, another concentration of six manors in south Shropshire, the tenancies of all of which were given to Walter by William fitzOsbern.[6] One of these was Stanton, and two others, Aldon and Stokesay, lay a short distance to the north. Coplestone-Crow argued, persuasively, that such a 'unique concentration of dominical power' suggests 'the existence of a major castle at Ludlow'. It is Walter de Lacy I, he reasoned, who is the most likely founder of Ludlow Castle, rather than his son Roger, to whom that title has traditionally been ascribed. This hypothesis is not inconsistent with the architectural evidence, which assigns the curtain wall of the inner bailey and the original gatehouse to 'the last quarter of the eleventh century'[7], with Renn suggesting a date of 'around 1080' for the wall arcade in the original entrance passage, with curling ornament on the capitals.[8] This view is endorsed by John Newman, who states in the revised edition of the *Shropshire* volume in the *Buildings of England* series that Walter probably began construction *c*.1070, i.e. while he was still a tenant of fitzOsbern.[9]

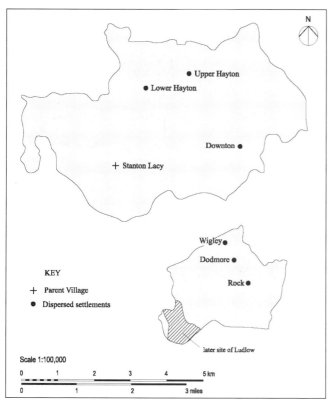

Fig. 12. *The manor of Stanton Lacy in 1086, showing early townships*

The Domesday Book survey of Stanton Lacy, 1085[10]

Walter de Lacy I died in 1085, supposedly by falling from a ladder at a church in Hereford, so that his son Roger is recorded as Lord of the de Lacy manors in the Domesday Book' record made during that year.[11] The Domesday survey shows that Stanton, with 22 hides (units of plough-able land), was the most productive manor in south Shropshire, though Bromfield was close behind with 20. The manor was well populated, with 70 villagers and 23 other residents, as well as 34 serfs.[12] Population estimates are hazardous, but a total of between 600 and 700 people has been postulated.[13]

Such a population could well have sustained a number of outlying settlements, as well as the core village around the parish church, the antiquity of which has already been considered.[15] Place name evidence suggests that some, at least, of the outlying hamlets,

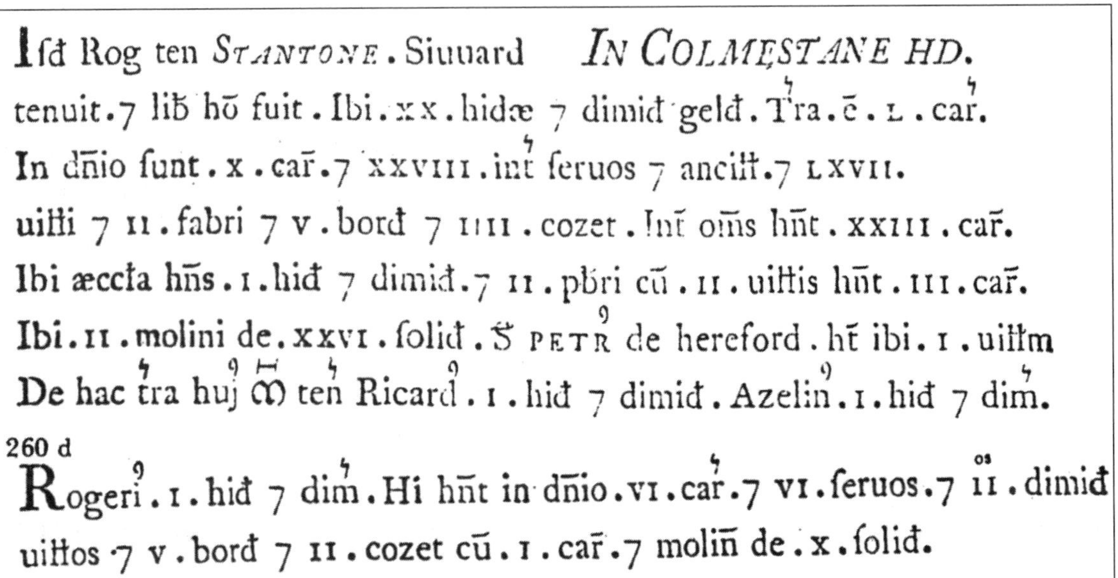

Iſđ Rog ten *STANTONE* . Siuuard   *IN COLMESTANE HD.*

tenuit.7 liƀ hõ fuit . Ibi . xx . hidæ 7 dimiđ geld . Tra . c̄ . ʟ . car.

In dn̄io funt . x . car̄ . 7 xxviii . in̄t feruos 7 ancilł . 7 ʟxvii.

uiłłi 7 ii . fabri 7 v . borđ 7 iiii . cozet . In̄t on̄s hn̄t . xxiii . car̄.

Ibi æccła hn̄s . i . hiđ 7 dimiđ . 7 ii . pƀri cū . ii . uiłłis hn̄t . iii . car̄.

Ibi . ii . molini de . xxvi . foliđ . S̄ ᴘᴇᴛʀ de hereford . hī ibi . i . uiłłm

De hac t̃ra huj ᴁ ten Ricarđ . i . hiđ 7 dimiđ . Azelin . i . hiđ 7 dim.

260 d

Rogeri . i . hiđ 7 dim . Hi hn̄t in dn̄io . vi . car̄ . 7 vi . feruos . 7 ii . dimiđ

uiłłos 7 v . borđ 7 ii . cozet cū . i . car̄ . 7 molin̄ de . x . foliđ.

In CULVESTONE Hundred

4 Roger also holds STANTON (Lacy). Siward held it; he was a free man. 20½ hides which pay tax. Land for 50 ploughs. In lordship 10 ploughs; 28 slaves, male and female;
67 villagers, 2 smiths, 5 smallholders and 4 Cottagers; between them they have 23 ploughs.
A church which has 1½ hides; 2 priests with 2 villagers have 3 ploughs.
2 mills at 26s.
St. Peter's of Hereford has 1 villager there.
Of this manor's land Richard holds 1½ hides, Azelin 1½ hides,

Roger 1½ hides. They have 6 ploughs in lordship and 6 slaves and 2 half-villagers, 5 smallholders and 2 Cottagers with 1 plough.
A mill at 10s.

Fig. 13. The text of the Stanton Lacy entry in The Domesday Book, with transcription[14]

all of which are listed by Eyton as in existence in the 13th century, are pre-1086 in origin, each with residents who accounted for some of the total population.[16] A major issue for this publication is whether there was such a small settlement on the future site of Ludlow, constituting the kind of 'concealed incipient town' which has been identified in Trentham parish in Staffordshire, later becoming Newcastle-under-Lyme.[17] The absence of a reference to the castle is not significant, for castles were not liable to tax – and the prime purpose of the Domesday survey was to record the potential for taxation.

The indications of economic specialisation in the Stanton Domesday record – two smiths and three mills – are those that would be found in any vibrant farming based rural economy, and give no hint of urbanisation. The number of 'slaves', 34, is large enough to include construction workers at the castle as well as agricultural workers on the demesne, but that has to be conjectural. Again, the presence of three riders – usually taken to be administrators with horses – is a sign of an active de Lacy involvement in the affairs of the manor, but not necessarily evidence of early urban development.

Another feature of the Stanton Domesday entry is the record of 'one church' and 'two priests'.[18] Priests are mentioned in only 42 of Shropshire's 485 Domesday manors, and in only half of these is a church also recorded. Many more churches than this are known to have existed in 1086, so the conclusion must be that Domesday, primarily a taxation record, includes churches and priests only when they are involved in manorial assets. There are only five manors in south Shropshire where two priests are listed, the others being Burford, Lydbury North, Morville, and Westbury – all of them, like Stanton, serving large tracts of agricultural land. At Stanton, a former minster church, it seems likely that the two priests were required to maintain the village church and to attend to the pastoral needs of the area, though this does not entirely rule out the possibility of a church at Ludlow, as was postulated in chapter 3.[19]

The second generation of de Lacy lords of Ludlow: Roger and Hugh I[20]
We are on certain ground, however, in tracing the short but violent career of Roger de Lacy, who rebelled twice against the king, now William II. The second rebellion, in 1095, led to his banishment from England the following year. Roger was succeeded as lord of the de Lacy estates by his brother Hugh de Lacy I, who held the lordship until his death before 1115. Little is known of Hugh. Wightman has suggested that 'the archaeological evidence

is not sufficiently precise to rule out the possibility that Hugh I built it [i.e. Ludlow Castle] after Roger's banishment in 1096',[21] while in 1108 he is known to have been involved in the foundation of Llanthony Abbey in Monmouthshire.

Payn fitzJohn, a rising man of ambition

A much stronger contender for initiating or extending the town of Ludlow is Payn fitzJohn, who succeeded Hugh de Lacy I as Lord. Payn, the son of an East Anglian baron, was a career civil servant who rose to prominence under Henry I, king from 1100-35.[22] 'A hard man who knew how to keep men loyal',[23] Henry governed by efficient administration, and nurtured people like Payn, later described as 'secretary and privy councillor of the king'.[24] About 1115, after Hugh de Lacy's death, Henry allowed Payn fitzJohn to marry Sybil, Hugh de Lacy I's daughter and heiress.[25] With Hugh de Lacy's younger brother, Walter de Lacy, following a religious calling – he became Abbot of St Peter's, Gloucester – Payn thus took possession of all the de Lacy estates in England. This was at the expense of Gilbert de Lacy, whom most authorities regard as the son of the banished Roger.[26]

Payn fitzJohn achieved great power on the Welsh border, becoming Sheriff of both Herefordshire and Shropshire during the 1120s, and later Justiciar (chief political officer and administrator of justice) of both counties. Among members of the early de Lacy family he seems a strong candidate for the promotion of a town, the likelihood of which is strengthened by the research of Coplestone-Crow. He has shown how Payn added to the de Lacy lands around Ludlow, increasing their 1086 values by 35%. This created, he argued, 'a powerful economic and military unit which served both his own purpose as a marcher lord and also that of the crown he served in his capacity of Sheriff and Justiciar'.[27] Coplestone-Crow could well have added that a new or enlarged town would have been a focal point of such an economic unit, but his detailed research concentrates on manorial tenure and knight's fees, and does not embrace urban developments. Though some dates need revision, Beresford listed over 20 new towns planted in England and Wales during the reign of Henry I, several of them on or near the Welsh border, so that development at Ludlow at this time would have been part of a wider regional pattern.[28]

Civil war, nationally and regionally

The death of Henry I in 1135 began a period of dynastic struggle for the English throne through the civil war between his daughter Matilda and his nephew Stephen. Payn hoped to secure the de Lacy estates for his heirs by a marriage contract between his daughter Cecily and Roger, Earl of Hereford, son of Miles of Gloucester (once a fellow civil servant). His claim, however, was contested by Gilbert de Lacy, who returned from exile after the death of Henry I.[29] After Payn's death in 1137, killed by an arrow whilst pursuing Welsh raiders, this local dispute became embroiled in the civil war. In 1138 Gervase Pagnal, an ally of Gilbert, held Ludlow Castle for Matilda, but in 1139 it was besieged and captured by Stephen, who then gave it to Joce de Dinan.[30]

The siege of Ludlow Castle by Stephen is a well known event, described by no fewer than eight medieval chroniclers. The earliest of these, and probably the most reliable, was Henry of Huntingdon, an East Anglian priest who became Archdeacon of Huntingdon and was asked by his bishop to write a history of England.[31] The first edition, written in 1129, was based on Bede and other early chroniclers, but later editions, issued up to 1154, cover contemporary events. Henry's description of the Ludlow siege reads:

> Having led Henry the son of the king of Scotland into England, (Stephen) attacked Lodelowe when the same Henry having been almost dragged from his horse by a grappling iron would have been captured had not the king himself bravely rescued him from his enemies.

This account of the siege of Ludlow, written within 15 years of the event, is much quoted by later writers because of its portrayal of Stephen's heroism, but its significance here is that it uses the place name 'Lodelowe' for the first time. That name must have been current when the chronicle was written, i.e. before 1154, and was probably in use in 1139 or earlier.

A much later chronicle, which can be conveniently cited here, is that of Melsa, an Abbey in east Yorkshire, which was compiled in the late 14th century by Abbot Burton, 'using ancient abstracts and parchments'.[32] These abstracts have been copied from earlier documents but though there is no clear cause to doubt their authenticity they are less reliable than contemporary accounts. Ludlow is one of seven places mentioned, but the reference is to the towns as well as to the castles, implying that the new town of 'Lodelowe', or part of it, was already in existence:

At which time certain magnates, opponents of the king and favourites of the empress, making way against King Stephen, occupied the castles and towns of Hereford, Bristol, Slede, Kerry, Ludlow, Oxford and Malton, as well as others besides, all of which however the same King Stephen afterwards recovered again.

Joce de Dinan and the Fitzwarine Romance: enigmas and uncertainties

The new lord of Ludlow, Joce de Dinan, is also of great importance in conjectures about the origins of Ludlow. He is thought to have been a Breton from north-west France, taking his name from the historic port of Dinan. After the Norman conquest, the family had settled at Hartland in Devon, but Joce had been drawn to the Marches through affinity with the Breton lords of Monmouth, an area where Hugh de Lacy had influence.[33] From there he entered Stephen's household and became a royal protege.[34] Much of what is known about him comes, however, from the Fitzwarine Romance, the enigmatic nature of which has been considered above (p. 8). The narrative describes the long running dispute between Joce, who is portrayed at first as the Lord and holder of Ludlow Castle, and the de Lacys who are seeking to recover it, though in the Romance the chief protagonist is called Walter, an honoured family name, rather than the historic Gilbert who was the de Lacys' actual enemy in the 1140s. The parts of the Romance which cast light on the growth of Ludlow are considered below, but it can be noted here that the castle is said eventually to have been captured by de Lacy. In reality, however, Joce seems to have given up the castle before his death, perhaps receiving lands in Berkshire in compensation.[35]

The Fitzwarine Romance gives detailed but sometimes puzzling descriptions of Ludlow topography. The most significant of these reads:

> And the town which is called Ludelowe was for a long time called Dynan. Under the town of Dynan this Joce caused to be built a bridge of stone and lime over the river at Temede, in the high road which runs through the March and from Chester to Bristol. Joce made his Castle with three baillies and encircled it with a double ditch the one within and other without. [36]

This passage poses many difficulties, but there is some architectural evidence that Ludford bridge has Norman origins.[37]

Gilbert de Lacy, a Knight Templar

The position of Gilbert de Lacy in the family pedigree is uncertain. Most authorities give him as the son of Roger de Lacy, though it is not known if he was born in England or in exile.[38] In genealogies of the Talbot family, however, he is given as the son of Emma, a sister of Roger, Hugh I and Walter the Abbot of Gloucester, Emma marrying Hugh de Talbot. If Gilbert was their son, he must have changed his name when exerting his claim through his mother to the de Lacy inheritance. He is said to have been born '*c*.1104', a date not inconsistent with his later career.[39]

Gilbert de Lacy enlisted in the Templars, a religious and military order who protected pilgrims and crusaders. He may have joined the Second Crusade in 1147, but he certainly went to Palestine in 1159, in 1163 becoming the preceptor of the Templars in Tripoli. He perhaps gained possession of Ludlow Castle from Joce *c*.1150, but soon surrendered this and other estates to his son, Hugh de Lacy II, who was said to have been in dispute with Joce de Dinan over lands in Herefordshire in 1154. It is often stated to have been Gilbert who determined the design of the round nave of the chapel of St Mary Magdalene in the inner bailey of Ludlow Castle, in which case that unusual building may date from the early 1150s. His preoccupations seem, however, to have been away from Ludlow, and he is not a strong contender for a lead role in developing the town.

Hugh de Lacy II, a known developer of towns, and his son Walter II

Hugh de Lacy II, on the other hand, is likely to have had a major impact on the Ludlow plan. Described by Giraldus as 'a swarthy man, small and ill made', he was a loyal supporter of Henry II, whose legal and administrative reforms brought order to England and created an economic climate in which many new towns were planted or expanded.[40] In 1165 he was probably present in the king's campaign against Owain Gwynedd in north Wales, but the climax of his career came in 1171, when he went with the king to Ireland. There he became Justiciar and Lord of Meath, enjoying at one time 'almost royal authority'. His activities in Ireland included town promotion and planning as at Drogheda, the plan of which Keith Lilley, then of London University, contrasts with Conzen's 'southern plan unit' at Ludlow, which he dates as 'probably some time in the 1160s'.[41]

It was probably Hugh de Lacy II who was the builder of the outer bailey of the castle, thereby quadrupling the area. It has sometimes been alleged that an early use of the outer bailey was to gather troops for the conquest of Ireland, which, if correct, suggests a date of about 1170.[42] Pevsner, in 1958, described this outer bailey as 'late 12th century', but Renn and Shoesmith brought this forward to 'before 1177', when the king, having granted de Lacy the lordship of Meath in Ireland, took Ludlow Castle into his own hands, installing Thurstan fitzSimon as custodian.[43] The dating of these events is significant because, as pointed out by St John Hope and others, the outer bailey probably truncated both Dinham and a corner of the 'southern plan unit', indicating that both were laid out earlier.[44] A final contribution from the time of Hugh de Lacy II to our understanding of the town plan comes through his gift of 12 burgages on the west side of the lower part of Corve Street to the Knights Hospitaller of Dinmore, a gift which is undated but which must have occurred before his murder in Ireland in 1186.[45] This shows that the lower part of Corve Street, and by implication the rest of the street, had been burgaged by this date, and also suggests that the furthest burgages from the town centre had not been settled at the time of the gift.

In 1186 Hugh de Lacy II was succeeded by his son, Walter de Lacy II, but Ludlow Castle remained in the king's hands until 1189, when Walter received livery, being therefore at least 21 years old.[46] At various times in the 1190s – 1194, 1198 and 1199 – the castle was taken back by the king because of Walter's misconduct, and again from 1210 to 1215. At other times, however, Walter was high in royal favour, as in 1216, when he was given charge of Hereford Castle and served as Sheriff of Herefordshire until 1223. Undated grants at Ludlow bearing his signature perhaps come from this period, or from 1226 to 1234, when there is no record of his being in Ireland. One grant, of the Hospital of St John in Lower Broad Street, was dated by Weyman as '*circa* 1221', and the other, of a pound of pepper corn as rent for an unidentified ditch, as 1229.[47]

The laws of Breteuil

These were the by-laws under which a number of Norman towns were governed, and which were instituted in England soon after the Conquest by William fitzOsbern.[48] They were employed at Hereford, the prime seat of fitzOsbern, and were copied at a number of other towns, including several on the Welsh border. They certainly prevailed under the later de Lacys, for when Walter de Lacy II, Earl of Meath and Lord of Trim from 1194 until his death in 1241, granted the laws of Breteuil to the borough of Drogheda, they were described as 'based on his borough of Ludlow'. The granting of burgages to burgesses for

12d a year was an important feature of the laws of Breteuil, so it is almost certain that they were current in Ludlow under the lordship of Hugh de Lacy II from the 1150s to 1186.

The laws of Breteuil conferred many privileges, consistent with the medieval dictum that 'town air breathes free'. Burgesses were allowed to marry without the intervention of a manorial lord; they were exempt from distant military service; they were free from tolls within the borough; they could buy, sell and bequeath burgages or parts of burgages without restraint. There are also signs of a corporate body, for if a burgage was vacant for a year or more, 'the Community' was answerable to the Lord for the rent. As Faraday observed, with 'several of these characteristics' operating in Ludlow, 'it is reasonable to suppose that most of them were established there'.[49]

Urban vitality in the late twelfth century

During the lordships of Hugh de Lacy II and Walter de Lacy I there are many references to Ludlow. These begin in 1169, but 12th-century records of towns are often sparse, and silence before that date does not necessarily mean inactivity. On no fewer than 34 occasions between 1176 and 1199 there are references to fines, trading practices and disputes over coinage at Ludlow, all indicating a busy and perhaps thriving community.[50] In 1190, 'the men of Ludlow' were charged £7 18s 4d to buy wheat, oats, pigs and wine to supply the castle, then in royal hands, an indication that an important function of Ludlow was to supply the garrison.[51] In the 1180s there are references to Herbert the Reeve, a suggestion of some measure of local government,[52] while the inclusion of seven burgesses surnamed Ludlow in the Dublin Roll of Burgesses in the late 12th-century implies that Ludlow men had followed Hugh de Lacy II on his Irish adventures – and that they were rewarded with grants of Dublin properties.[53]

The enlargement and rebuilding of the parish church in 1199, with a new bell tower erected in 1200, is a further indication of growth. The alleged discovery of the bones of Irish saints has been considered in chapter 3 but the need for enlarging the church at this time is relevant to this chapter. The original dedication of the church was to St Philip and St James as well as to St Laurence, and though Philip and James had been dropped by 1284 or earlier, the fair on their festival, 1st May, continued for much of the Middle Ages and almost certainly had 12th-century origins, another sign of early urban vitality.[54] The charters enabling these fairs have been lost, the earliest survivor for Ludlow being that of 1461.[55]

Another sign of growth and status was the existence by 1200 of two schools, probably a grammar school and a choir school.[56] Even more indicative of the success of the new town is the document which refers to the schools: an injunction from Herbert Walter, Archbishop of Canterbury, relating to a dispute about tithes between the 'parson' and 'vicar' of Ludlow.[57] The document, crucially, shows that Ludlow was already a parish and had probably been so for a number of years, with a Rector – 'governor or head priest' (called parson) – and his deputy, the vicar, a substitute or *vicarious*. The Rector was supported by various rights, including glebe land and tithes, a tenth of most kinds of produce from the land, a small portion of which he could assign to the vicar.[58] The vicar, 'our dear son Philip, priest', claimed that he had held his cure 'for some time in peace and quiet'.[59] The parson, probably non-resident, was Geoffrey de Lacy, perhaps a protege of the de Lacys who adopted the family surname. Some new towns had to wait many years to attain a parish with its own tithes and other rights and privileges. Newport in Shropshire, for example, was an early 12th-century royal foundation in the parish of Edgmond. There are references to a church from 1129 but full parish status was not obtained until 1221. The early acquisition of parish status at Ludlow is a measure of the town's success and of the influence of its promoters. Once fixed, the parish boundaries are unlikely to have been changed until the 19th century because of the difficulties of altering tithes, a situation that has caused one author to observe: 'The canon law laid its cold hand on the parishes of Europe and froze the pattern.'[60] It can be assumed, therefore, that the Ludlow parish boundary of later centuries was in place by 1200, and that it had been drawn advisedly, to mark the limits of an area that was recognisably urban.

The town defences

The stone wall and ditch which surrounded the core of Ludlow, with the seven gates that gave controlled access in and out of the town, are a prominent feature, substantial parts of which survive today. In his scholarly *The Walls and Gates of Ludlow: Their Origins and Early Days* (1999), Train uses murage grants and other evidence to date the construction of these features to the second half of the 13th century, which is beyond the period covered in the current publication. However, because the walls may have followed the line of earlier defences, they are relevant to this study, and some of the issues and difficulties raised by Train will be considered in chapter 5.

People of Ludlow before and around 1200

Towns exist and grow for the people who live in them, so this chapter concludes with a survey of what is known about the first Ludlow residents. The expanding town plan implies a growing population. There is no reliable means of estimating Ludlow's population before 1377, for which year Faraday, by extrapolation from the Poll Tax return, suggested 'about 1,725'.[61] Noting the plagues and other disasters of the 14th century, however, he believed that earlier population totals were higher, citing a possible 2,000 in 1300. If, as this study has argued, the town had reached its full physical extent by 1200, the total then could have already been approaching that figure, Faraday himself reminding us that, in the country at large, 'the period 1150 to 1300 was a time of huge population increase'.

The names of the lords of Ludlow and of some of their relatives are well known and have been cited, with slight variations, by several writers and in previous chapters of this study. Also known are some of the lesser landowners in Stanton (Lacy) in 1086: Richard, Roger, Azelin and Auti, though not all of these were necessarily residents.[62] The Fitzwarine Romance gives the names of some persons supposedly then in Ludlow Castle, including the ill-fated Mariana de Bruer, who threw herself from the battlements when she discovered the treachery of her lover, Sir Ernauld de Lis; but their existence cannot be authenticated.[63] The Pipe Rolls, with references to Ludlow intermittently from 1167, and other documents, name a number of people trading or involved in financial transactions. These included William de Munchanesi, probably a merchant, who was rich enough in 1198 to lend money to Walter de Lacy II;[64] and Norman de Swineton, described as 'servant' but perhaps a lawyer, who negotiated a house purchase on behalf of the owner, Maud de Mesac, who was 'not in England'.

Compared with the numerous Ludlow residents named in documents after 1200, these are but a small selection. It is disappointing, too, but not necessarily significant, that none of them have the locative and occupational surnames that Faraday was able to analyse for the 1250-1300 period. He showed that of people on a Palmers' Guild rental from about 1270, 35% have locative surnames, which when plotted on a map showed that 57% of that number came from within 10 miles of Ludlow and another 25% from between 10 and 20 miles.[65] There is no reason to doubt that a comparable number of 12th century migrants into Ludlow came from similar distances, though the possibility of some settlers coming from more distant de Lacy manors, as Ludlow burgesses went to Dublin in the 1170s, must not be discounted. Some of the great trading dynasties certainly began their Ludlow careers very early in the 13th century if not earlier. For example, by 1210 Andrew, son of Milo, a cloth merchant who owned land in the vicinity, was beginning to acquire property in Ludlow.[66] Other chance references from the early 13th century also catch early pulsations of commercial life, as in 1204 when a Richard Falconer was a lodger 'at the house of Adelina de Ludlow', the first reference we have to a Ludlow inn.[67]

Chapter 5

Streets and Plots, plan analysis of early Ludlow

This chapter begins by defining 'plan analysis' and reviewing the nature of burgage plots and their occurrence at Ludlow. It then examines the pattern of streets and plots in the suggested plan units, using a modified system from that introduced by Conzen in 1966. For each unit a 1:2500 OS map extract from the 1884 edition is provided, accompanied by a reconstruction of the street and burgage pattern of 1619.[1] The units come together to form what Slater and others have called 'a composite town plan'.[2]

The chapter continues with some comments on the size of the burgaged area and finishes with a postscript on the walls and gates of the town. These took their present form in the 13th century and are therefore beyond the scope of the present study, but a consideration of their evolution has implications for the period under review.

Plan Analysis and Burgage Plots

In his epic work on *Alnwick, Northumberland*: *A Study in Town-Plan Analysis*, published in 1960,[3] Conzen defined a town plan as having three distinct complexes of elements:

1. Streets and their arrangement in a street-system;
2. Plots and their aggregation in street blocks; and
3. Buildings or, more precisely, their block plans

This chapter, dealing principally with the 12th century, considers streets and plots, though buildings, except occasionally, are beyond the scope of this publication. The technique used is that which Conzen and others have called *plan analysis*, that is the deductions which can be reasonably made from later large scale plans and from field measurements. Plan analysis has been impressively used by a number of historical geographers, including Slater at Lichfield and Bond at Thame.[4] With documentary references so sparse for Ludlow in the 12th century, plan analysis is the only means available to supplement the chronological framework already established.

At Ludlow most plots were burgages, as in many other towns, including those boroughs which observed the Laws of Breteuil.[5] These are the cells from which medieval towns were constructed. As emphasised above, the right to hold one or more burgage was a valued privilege of a 'burgess', a town dweller who was 'free' of the feudal restrictions of rural manors.

Over the last thirty years, the Ludlow Historical Research Group has done prolific work on the Ludlow burgages, and a detailed survey of these is in preparation for publication. The purpose here is to explain enough about the plots and their dimensions as is necessary to cast light on the early development of the town. The prime documentary sources are the 1619 rental of burgage rents payable to the Corporation, which records all freehold properties in street sequence[6]; and the 1592 rental of properties owned by the Corporation, which also follows street sequences.[7] The two documents mesh together to form property grids which can be supplemented from other sources. From these grids it has been possible to superimpose a map of Ludlow burgages in 1619 on a plan derived from maps available in the 19th century, thus providing a base for plan analysis that is two and a half centuries earlier than the sources used by other scholars. Earlier burgage rentals, dated 1561[8], 1482[9] and 1470[10], though none of them embrace the whole town, enable the ownership of many properties to be taken back to the 15th and 14th centuries, while from the earliest rentals of the Palmers Guild the ownership of some properties can to be traced to the 13th century.[11] All the evidence suggests that the burgage pattern was essentially that laid out by the first plantations, except for subsequent amalgamations and divisions, many of which are documented. The pattern has flexibility, with some burgages added as late as the 15th century, but a total of just over 500 burgages can be identified in the historic town using documentary and cartographic evidence. In spite of later distortions, a large number of medieval plots, some of them probably from the original laying out of the town, survived until the 17th century, and most of these can be detected on the 1884 OS maps of the town, with a number surviving unaltered to the present day. Nos. 1 and 3 Market Street, shown on Fig. 17, are fine examples of modern properties that retain their original dimensions, each being three perches (49½ feet) wide.

As in several other towns, many plots had measurements which are multiples of the pole or perch, 16½ feet. Of 515 plots, 376 (73%) had widths which were multiples of a perch or fractions of a perch, the most common widths being a perch itself (42), one and a half perches (36), two perches (91) and three perches (42).[12] The lengths of the plots showed yet more accord with the perch, 453 (88%) having lengths which are perch multiples, the most common length being 16 perches (35). It will be shown, however, that a minority of plots, including some that appear to be original, did not have perch dimensions, while Slater has reminded us that the areas of plots also have to be considered.[13]

The Castle and Dinham

Though, as Lilley argues, 'the area of the castle and Dinham are morphologically distinct', together they form 'a unified part of Ludlow's town plan', which logically should be considered first.[14] Much of the original nature of the unit, however, has been distorted by the creation of the outer bailey of the castle, probably about 1170.[15] It will be suggested that the castle and Dinham had their own defence system from an early date, possibly the late 11th century.

The most striking feature of this early defence system is a wide, entrenched ditch, later known as Christ Croft, aligned along part of the eastern flank of Dinham. This is shown on Fig. 14. It was originally called 'fossatum', the Latin word commonly used for a defensive ditch.[16] It was demesne (manorial) land, as town ditches usually were, but there is no evidence that this continued south of what is now Camp Lane, though a field boundary, slightly angled, continues the line of Christ Croft to the River Teme. St John Hope and others have postulated that a northern extension of Christ Croft was truncated when the outer bailey was built,[17] while its alignment with what is now Castle House can also be noted. These matters could be verified by archaeological excavation, but this has not yet happened, to the regret of the late Philip Barker[18] and others. It would be logical to expect the whole of Christ Croft to be demesne, but the 1470 and later rentals show that the property at the north end of the ditch, F251 (now Nos. 11 and 12 Dinham), was freehold, a puzzling anomaly, with an unrecorded sale of the demesne land being the most likely explanation.[19]

The morphology of a possible pre-Norman Dinham must remain speculative, but the oldest component which can be identified with certainty is the castle's inner bailey, which may date, as argued above, from the 1070s.[20] It is a 'ringwork'[21] that is elliptical in shape, with four flanking towers along its western and north-western sides, overlooking the precipitous

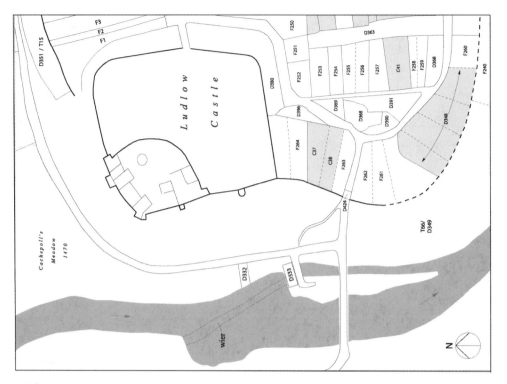

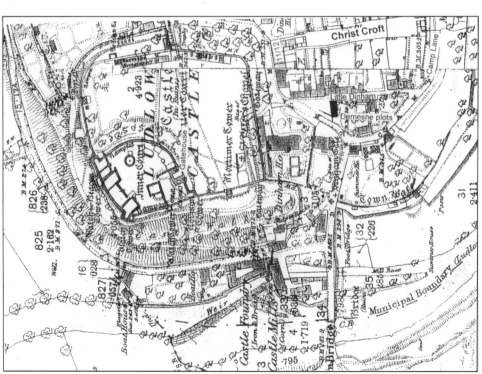

Fig. 14. The castle and Dinham, perhaps an integrated unit with early defences: OS 1884 extract with identified burgages of 1619 and other features

50

slope which makes the castle a fine defensive site. As pointed out by Renn, the original gatehouse, later raised to what has been called 'the gatehouse keep', faces just east of south, directly in line with the open space that is now at the centre of Dinham, providing a site for St Thomas's Chapel.[22]

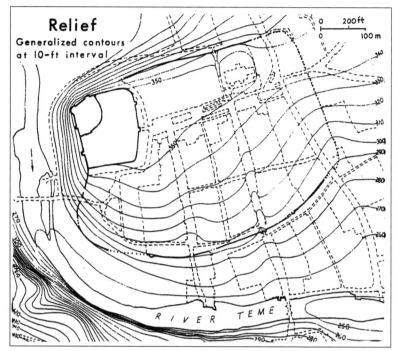

Fig.15. The line of defences on the south west of Ludlow, shown in relation to contours (after Train, 1999, pp.24-25)

Train, in The *Walls and Gates of Ludlow* (1999), argued convincingly that the town wall, which swung west from near the south end of Christ Croft, followed the line of earlier defences, rather than taking the most direct route along the 290 foot contour.[23]

The wall, and these earlier defences, dropped obliquely down the contours to 260 feet, before turning sharply north to climb to the castle at 340 feet, thereby enclosing a larger space than would otherwise have been the case.

Conzen (1988) described the early settlement at Dinham as 'an agricultural settlement, sharing the rural atmosphere of the surrounding countryside', with plots that were 'archaic looking, large and squat'.[24] This description referred, presumably, to the fan-shaped series of plots, some of them 3 perches wide and 11 perches deep, along the western and south-western edges of Dinham to-day, some of which have been amalgamated to form the grounds of Dinham House and Dinham Lodge. The 15th century burgage rentals show that there were then more burgages occupying the land between Camp Lane and the postulated town wall, and continuing as far as the sunken Christ Croft.[25] Further north, beyond what is now Dinham House, the western burgage series may have continued into what later became the outer bailey, again indicating a target for archaeology. The shorter plots on the east side of what was later called Little Dinham or St Thomas's Lane are, Conzen suggested, a later series of burgages, developed at the same time as 'the middle and southern plan unit', which lay east of Christ Croft.[26]

Lilley (1997) presented an impressive list of Norman castle towns, each with a market place and a church.[27] The suggested embryonic settlement at Dinham can be shown to conform to this model, an alternative view to Conzen's 'village'. The open space north of St Thomas's chapel may be the remnant of the original market place, which perhaps extended northwards into what became the outer bailey. The chapel itself has Norman features inside a later casing, and has traditionally been dated as post-1172, the year of Thomas's martyrdom.[28] Parts of the building may, however, be older, particularly the archaic south wall, which one architectural historian believes to be 'late Saxon' in style, though not necessarily built until after the Norman Conquest.[29] Faraday, too, suggests that there may have been 'a simple chapel on

Fig. 16. The south elevation of Dinham Chapel, showing early archaeological features which may pre-date the dedication to St Thomas after his death in 1172

the same site' before the present building was erected.[30] South of the chapel, demesne land was divided into irregular plots, the shapes of which are still apparent.[31] Excavation in 1973 confirmed that the nave of the original chapel was west of the present arched entrance, which implied that the road beside the chapel was also originally further west. [32]

The integrated unit suggested is shown in its totality in Fig. 14. It is bounded on the north and north-west by the castle walls, those of the outer bailey perhaps following the line of earlier defences. These defences continued south-west, following the course detailed by Train and marked on Fig. 15. Christ Croft itself, reaching north along the line of Castle House, continued the defence along the vulnerable east flank, which lacked the outlying protection from the River Teme which was available in other directions.

The resultant enclosed area contained three defended areas. In the north was the inner bailey, with curtain walls built in the later 11th century. To the east and south was the outer bailey, laid out, it is suggested, before 1170, but perhaps following an extension of Christ Croft along its eastern side. Finally, the most southerly and largest of the enclosed spaces embraced the area that is now residential Dinham, bounded by Christ Croft on the east and Train's postulated defences to the south-west.

It is tempting to identify these three enclosed spaces with the 'three baillies' described in the Fitzwarine Romance, though the additional statement that 'Joce encircled it with a double ditch the one within and the other without' needs some examination. Writing in the early 14th century[33], the chronicler must have used local tradition and folk memory to recall the time when the settlement 'called Dynan' did exist as a separate entity with its 'three baillies' and its own defensive system, though it is unlikely to have assumed this format until the outer bailey was built c.1170, a generation after the events described supposedly took place. The 'two ditches' rather than three may have been an error in this tradition, perhaps arising from the 1250s, when 'The Friars of St Augustine' had 'their dwelling space' in Christ Croft, prior to 1256 when 'they first dwelt in Galdeford'.[34]

Finally in this section, it is appropriate to cite again the parallels with other Norman boroughs on the Welsh border, especially with the de Lacy borough of Longtown.(see p. 19).[35] As argued by Train:

> It is tempting to think that in the remains which time has allowed to survive in the remote village of Longtown one may be able to see the skeleton of the settlement which lies beneath the western end of Ludlow today.[36]

The High Street tract

The High Street tract is the term used by Conzen for what he identified as the original High Street, which ran eastwards from the castle to the Bull Ring, together with the 'deep' north-south burgages on either side, and the chequer-like space occupied by the church and the churchyard.[37] Parts of what Conzen described as 'a generously proportioned' market place were colonised by later rows and encroachments, but the western end, now Castle Square, retains its original spaciousness. From the present castle entrance to the Bull Ring the High Street tract measures just over 300 yards, but, as St John Hope argued, the original street was probably longer, having been truncated when the outer bailey was built, perhaps before 1171, as suggested above.[38] Such a market place, described by Conzen as 'generously proportioned', would have been longer though narrower than the 'great Market' at Bury St Edmunds, thought to have been laid out before 1086;[39] and both longer and wider than the High Street at Bridgnorth, an early 12th century foundation, which retains its original proportions.[40] It is tempting to see the plantation of such a market place at Ludlow as a promotion by the ambitious and powerful Payn fitzJohn, which would date it between 1115 and 1135.

The tract had a well preserved series of large burgages on its northern side, originally stretching to the line of the later town wall, though most are now truncated by the car park. Those in the west are 21 perches long, and terminate at the top of the steep slope overlooking Linney, which provided a natural line of defence. These large plots perhaps reflect a high level of economic activity by the first settlers, as farmers, craftsmen or merchants. Those in the east are shorter, and are truncated by burgages abutting to what is now College Street, though these too conform to perch multiples. Most of the burgages fronting the original High Street on the north side were three perches wide, but one (C22, now 10 Church Street), near the eastern end, was two perches, while three others (F7-9, now 8-12 Castle Street) were 31 feet wide. Further east, the church chequer, though later masked by encroachment, originally fronted the High Street. South of the original High Street, the burgages are less well preserved, perhaps by shortening or defacement when the southern plan unit was laid out at a later date, Conzen (1988) describing them as 'stunted and deformed'.[41] The best survivals are F192 and F193 (Nos. 1 & 2 and 3 & 4 Market Street), both of which are 3 perches wide and 10 perches deep. Shorter but well preserved north-south plots occur between Dinham and Mill Street (C45 and C46 & 47, now Castle Lodge) and at the eastern end of what is now Pepper Lane.

*Fig.17. The High Street tract: OS 1884 extract
with identified burgages of 1619 and earlier*

Later colonisation of the High Street market place

The colonisation or infilling of an original market place by later rows of stalls is a well-known historical process, of which Ludlow is a well attested example. As Bond and Aston showed of the Bishops of Lincoln at Thame in 1221, this was not a casual process but an initiative to increase demesne revenue.[42] The western end of Ludlow's huge market place was left open in the Middle Ages, though the first of a series of market halls had been built by the 16th century. Further east came 'the rows'. The two northern rows were 'the Butchers Rows' or 'the shambles', with a narrow lane between them later called Harp Lane.[43] Most of the 'selda', as the small shops were called in the late 13th century, were 11 foot square, paying 4d burgage rent a year. To the south, between what are now High Street and Market Street, was Baron's Row, with selda for which some rents, at least, were being paid in cumin seed in 1255.[44] Cumin seed became popular as rent in the reign of King John (1199-1216), which may suggest an early 13th-century origin for Baron's Row.

On the site of the present Butter Cross was another row of shops which were acquired at an early date by the Palmers' Guild, and near here also stood the original High Cross, facing down Broad Street at the hub of the medieval town.[45] Further east, as argued below, the street was probably narrowed by encroachment from the south; and further east again the

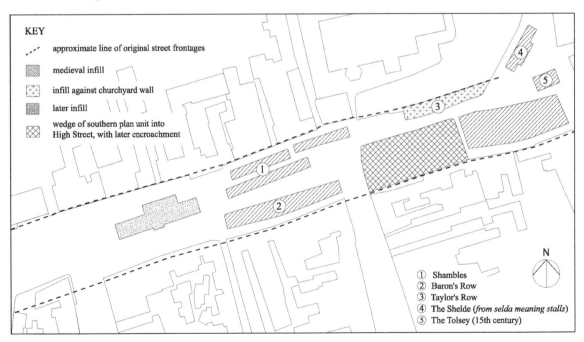

KEY

- - - approximate line of original street frontages

medieval infill

infill against churchyard wall

later infill

wedge of southern plan unit into High Street, with later encroachment

① Shambles
② Baron's Row
③ Taylor's Row
④ The Shelde (*from selda meaning stalls*)
⑤ The Tolsey (15th century)

N

Fig. 18. Colonisation of the High Street market place, showing infill and encroachment

street reached its narrowest point when a row of selda against the churchyard wall, known in the 13th century as 'Tailors' Row', protruded into the street from the north. These shops eventually encroached onto the churchyard, as evidenced by the human bodies which were excavated in 1994.[46] These bodies must have been buried here before the encroachment occurred.

East of Fish Street the street opens out again, round the triangular space once called 'the Beaste market', now the Bull Ring. In the north was a diagonally placed row known as 'the Shelde',[47] a derivation from the Latin *selda*, which probably took its alignment from the edge of the churchyard; while to the south an imposing row of buildings (Nos. 41-46 Bull Ring and 11-12 King Street) is separated from the original edge of the High Street market place by what is now Pepper Lane, but which in the 13th century was called 'the row behind the smiths'.[48] There was also a conduit house in the Beaste Market, next to which the Tolsey was later built as a courtroom.[49]

Units along the ancient north-south routeway

In this part of the town, Conzen (1968) considered only 'Bull Ring and Old Street and their burgage series', that formed 'an eastern unit' which he located entirely within the walls.[50] Hindle (1981) extended the unit as 'burgage plots along the Corve Street-Old Street route, perhaps as far south as the River Teme'.[51] Later (1990) he labelled the whole length of Corve Street as a 'linear market'.[52] Slater (1990), more perceptively, distinguished between 'the older tofts and crofts of Old Street', 'the market place at the east end of the church' and 'the newly planted burgage properties of Corve Street'.[53] Lilley (1997) put Old Street, Bull Ring and their plots together as his Unit I, added Holdgate Fee as Unit VIII, and recognized Corve Street as far north as what became the site of the Lower Gate as Unit IX; but gave no supporting explanation or commentary.[54]

Plan analysis shows clearly the distinctiveness of Corve Street and its burgages. The plots form a classic 'bilateral ribbon development' burgage series, with plots on each side of the street, many of them exactly 18 perches deep.[55] Some, however, deviate from this norm, especially in the north-west, where 12 burgages were given to the Knights Hospitaller of Dinmore by Hugh de Lacy II before 1186, though reduced in length by Corve Street lying near to the River Corve.[56] In the middle of the street the burgages consistently conform to a two perch width, though there is variation south and north. To the south, outside what became

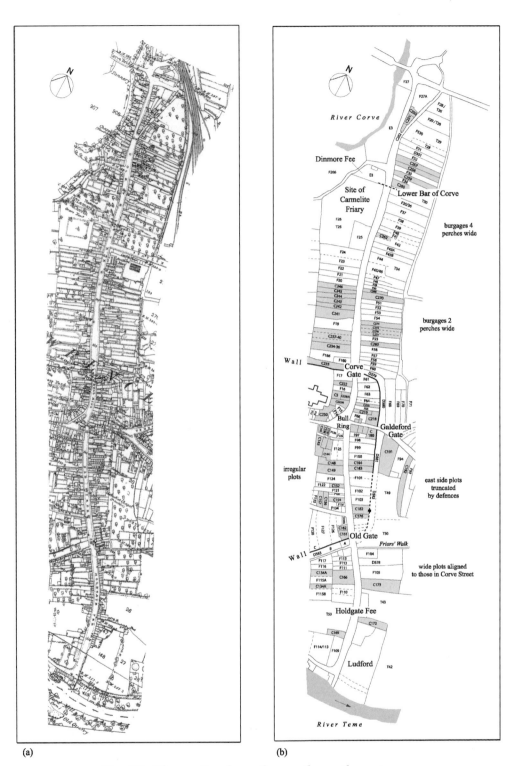

Fig. 19. Plan units along the north-south routeway:
(a) OS 1884 map extract and (b) identified burgages of 1619 and later, and other features

the site of Corve Gate, several burgages on the west side were originally 2½ perches wide, though there have been subsequent amalgamations; while to the north, between what are now Nos. 22 and 134 (F22 and F48), and the later site of lower Corve Gate, the original burgage width was four perches, though again there has been later distortion. Outside the lower Gate of Corve on the east side, the plots were less than 2 perches wide, perhaps reflecting a later phase of development.

The plots abutting Old Street and the Bull Ring are more enigmatic. It is tempting to see the three large plots, which are exactly or approximately 18 perches deep, on the east side of Holdgate Fee as a remnant of what was originally the continuation of the Corve Street series down the east side of Old Street. The Old Street burgages on the east side may have been truncated when the wall and ditch were constructed, some of them, e.g. F 103 (now No. 51), originally reaching to the western edge of the burgages on the south side of Lower Galdeford. On the west side of Old Street, the plots are very varied in size, some of them being very large, e.g. F123 (Nos. 24 to 26), which has an area of nearly a rood, whereas others are much smaller, e.g. C153 (No. 34), just over nine perches long and exactly one perch wide. The pattern, it can be argued, has a primeval, archaic appearance, and may reflect the pre-Norman 'crofts and tofts' postulated by Slater.[57]

The Bull Ring is necessarily a confused area where, it is contended, the eastern end of the High Street tract intermeshed with whatever plot pattern there may have been from earlier development. The presence of the Tolsey from the early 15th century and the later place name 'the Beaste market' support Slater's suggestion that the present Bull Ring, situated east of the church, was an early market place, though it is clear that many other Ludlow streets also had a market function.[58] The sharp break of slope between the burgages west of the Bull Ring and the churchyard suggest that the former were cut out of steeply sloping land.

The central and southern plan unit (see Figs. 20 and 21, pp. 60 and 61)
The special character of this area was recognised by St John Hope, who wrote of 'the wide thoroughfares' running south from 'the original High Street', of the narrow streets between them and of redundant streets east of Broad Street and west of Mill Street.[59] Conzen (1966) coined the phrase 'a central and southern plan unit' which contained 'Broad Street, Mill Street and their associated burgage series, with internal back and cross lanes'.[60] The unit, he wrote in 1966, represented 'a more advanced style of planning',[61] but in 1988 he called

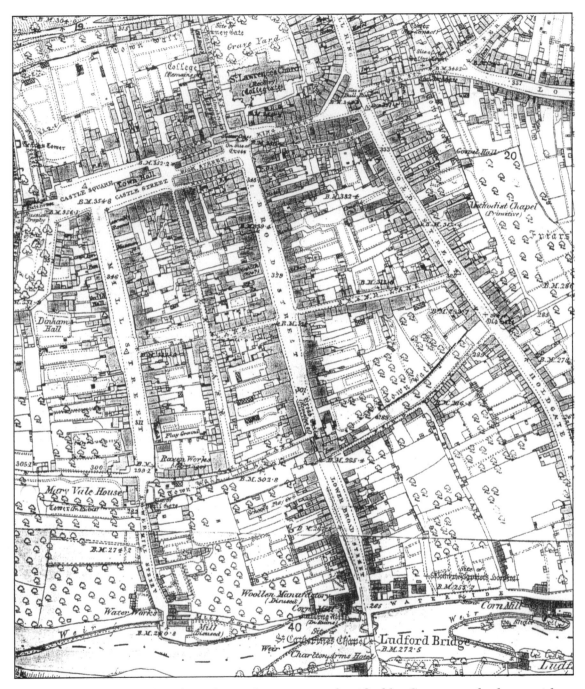

Fig. 20. The central and southern plan unit, as identified by Conzen and others, with adjoining parts of Ludlow: OS 1884 map extract

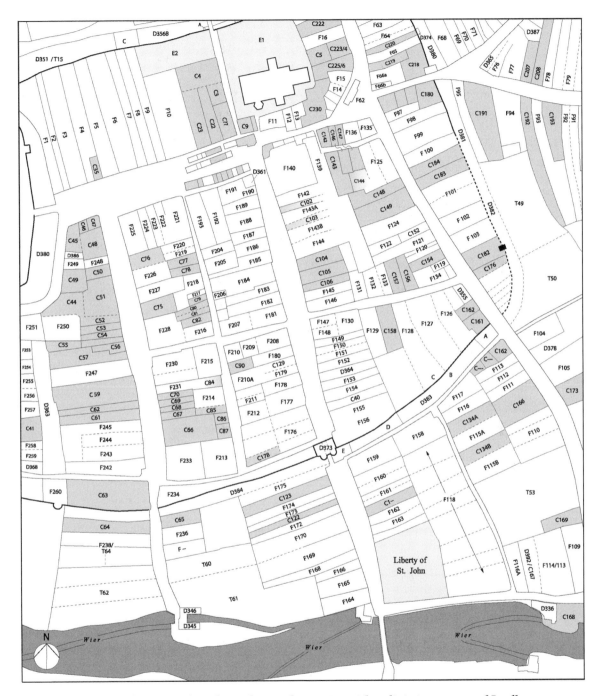

*Fig. 21. The central and southern plan unit, with adjoining parts of Ludlow:
identified burgages and others.*

it 'a major innovation of medieval town planning', which he attributed to the 13th century, pointing out a possible link with the bastides of Gascony.[62] Lilley (1997) repeated that 'a new area of streets and plots was laid out', with a form that was 'very regular, with streets intersecting at right angles and configured in a grid-iron plan', a plan form which he described as 'orthogonal'.[63]

The relative importance of the north-south streets varied. Their size, position and the frequency of early references indicate that Broad Street and Mill Street were the most important, each with a continuation beyond the walls as Lower Broad Street and Lower Mill Street. The former, with Ludford Bridge at its southern end, became the earliest mill site on the River Teme. The cigar shape of these streets is especially apparent in Broad Street and perhaps indicates an early market function, expanding down the hill from the High Street tract. The other north-south streets were narrower, but only one of these, Raven Lane – initially called 'the Narrow Lane' – is still a street. Its line is continued south of the town wall by a property boundary, along which house foundations were excavated during the building of Ludlow College Sports Hall in 1993.[64] Christ Croft in the west, probably a defensive ditch originally,[65] may have become another street when the middle and southern plan unit was laid out, but its cross-section was probably distorted by the excavating of clay in the 16th century.[66] Property boundaries suggest that there was another street in the east, between Broad Street and Old Street. This led southwards from Fish Street and terminated as St John's Road but was truncated by the constructing of the town wall and ditch and by the laying out of Brand Lane.

The lanes now called Brand Lane and Bell Lane, but which in early title deeds bore the common name of 'le Barndelone', perhaps after a barn building, are a classic cross-lane of the kind often found in 'bastide' towns. There is no evidence, however, of a continuation further west, as suggested by St John Hope.[67] The other cross lanes – St John's Lane, Silk Mill Lane and Camp Lane – are perhaps not in their original positions, due to displacement by the town walls. Within the grid, nearly all the burgages run approximately east to west, at right angles to the main streets. Exceptions are some of the plots adjoining Brand Lane and Bell Lane, especially those running south from Brand Lane to the town wall. Other exceptions occurred at Temeside, though west of St John's Lane an east-west pattern prevailed.

For most of the unit there seem to have been two series of burgages within each original property block. This is most apparent between Lower Broad Street and Holdgate Fee, where the survival of St John's Lane allowed easy access to the two inner series. Between Lower Broad Street and Lower Mill Street traces of short burgages can be seen, though on the upper part of the west side of Lower Broad Street longer plots are in place, perhaps formed by amalgamation. As late as 1669 the Burgage Rental referred to two burgages (F167) 'lying in a close by the river side', which seem to be part of a lost series.[68] West of Lower Mill Street all trace of the early burgage pattern had disappeared when the first maps were made, but medieval title deeds show that there were two blocks of burgages, with references to a lane leading to the inner block. Slater has used the west side of Lower Broad Street to hypothesise by metrological measurement that there were originally four blocks of land ownership, with widths of respectively 2, 6, 4 and 4 perches, which then sub-divided into smaller properties, some of which conformed to perch measurements, whereas others did not.[69]

North of the walls, the earliest known property boundaries suggest that the pattern was similar, though the convergence of Broad Street and Old Street towards the Bull Ring forced some compression. The pattern is most uniform between Broad Street and Mill Street, where the divide between two series of burgages, one abutting to Narrow Lane, the other to Broad Street or Mill Street, can often be clearly seen. Well documented cases include the four burgages held by William Barnaby in 1482, two of them in the Narrow Lane (F213), two in Mill Street (F233).[70] Burgage length is approximately 6 perches throughout, and a standard 3 perch width survives in places, especially to the east side of Mill Street above Bell Lane. It has been suggested by Slater (1990), however, that the division of these blocks was originally into large sub-blocks, with further sub-division on complex mathematical principles.[71]

Such holdings can certainly be identified from documentary sources. In the block between Mill Street, Bell Lane, Raven Lane and Castle Street, for example, the 1470 burgage rental identifies five properties in the north east as having been in the ownership of 'Hawkins'.[72] This is probably the John Hawkins who was involved in an ownership dispute of 1359, when the property was described as having been in 1320 'a tenement with eleven messuages and two shops'.[73] Slater also shows how blocks such as this were divided into plots with length and breadth ratios of 6:5, 10:3 and 12:2.5, all of which were of equal area though of different proportions. The 'plot arrangement is', he affirmed, one of 'great subtlety' which matches the advanced nature of the overall plan of the Mill Street/Broad Street unit, comparable in essence with the planning of mid-12th century Lichfield, though the street plan there is 'very different'.[74] Lilley put this into context by showing that knowledge of geometry underlay this

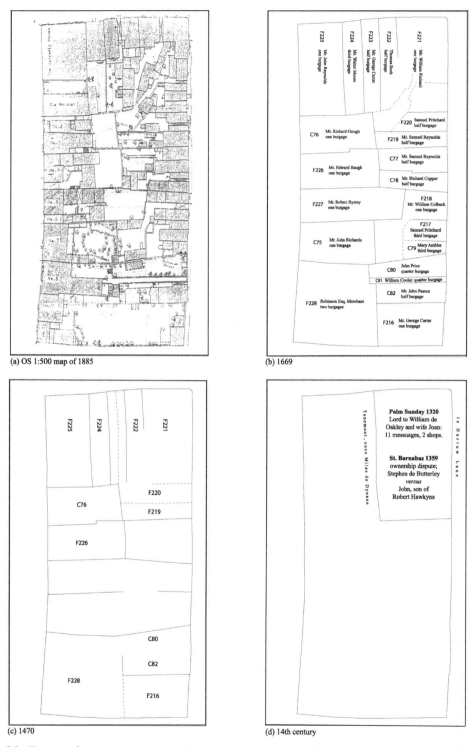

(a) OS 1:500 map of 1885

(b) 1669

(c) 1470

(d) 14th century

Fig. 22. Tenurial reconstruction of parts of the block of properties between Mill Street, Castle Street, Raven Lane and Bell Lane

kind of planning, citing the work of Adelard of Bath, an internationally known scholar who translated Euclid's *Elements* from Arabic into Latin, probably in *c*.1140.[75] This and other works, Lilley showed, 'became incorporated into the practice' of some surveyors, and could have influenced town planning.

East of Broad Street a standard burgage length is also apparent, where the original plots were eight perches long, though some were later extended eastwards into what is postulated as a redundant north-south street, running south from Fish Street. It is possible that short burgages abutted to this redundant street on its eastern side, F122 being the only survivor, as well as what are now the long burgages running west from Old Street. The straight western edge of these burgages clearly demarcates one side of the supposed redundant street, but the western side of that street is less regular, due to absorption into the Broad Street burgages. South of Brand Lane, the Broad Street burgages lengthen to 11 perches, part of a general expansion permitted by the divergence of Old Street. The burgages abutting to Old Street are very short, while between the two series long properties run from Brand Lane to the town wall, probably superimposed on an earlier pattern.

The fusion of the 'central and southern plan unit' with 'the High Street tract' can be perceived by plan analysis. As considered above,[76] some of the longer north-south properties abutting onto the south side of the High Street market place are probably survivors from an earlier planning phase. In other cases, for example at the top of Broad Street on the west side, these may have been overlaid and replaced by east-west burgages of the new unit. East of the street, at the top end, the new unit seems to have driven a wedge into the former High Street, which led eventually, after further encroachment, to the narrow King Street of to-day. On all these points, however, Slater was sceptical, and suggested alternatively that the High Street Tract and the Broad Street-Mill Street unit were laid out as one phase.[77]

Peripheral burgages within what became the parish boundary
Few of the previous writers on Ludlow's origins have said much about Galdeford. Of Ludlow's plan units, Conzen (1966) mapped Galdeford among his 'later components';[78] Hindle, without giving his reasons, dated its development as 'after 1260' or 'uncertain';[79] while Lilley demarcated the area between the town ditch and what became Friars' Walk as 'Plan Unit VIII'.[80] Yet the burgage pattern has every cartographic appearance of antiquity, while late 13th century rentals and title deeds show at least two generations of previous ownership.[81]

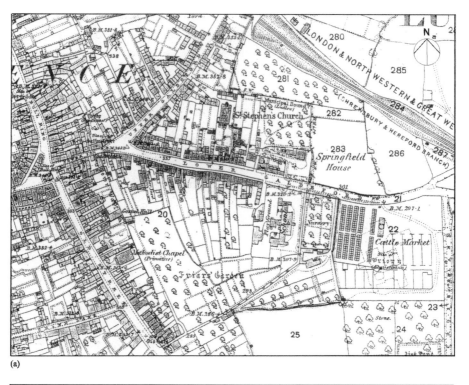

(a)

(b)

Fig. 23. Upper and Lower Galdeford, with adjoining parts of the Bull Ring and Old Street: OS 1884 map extract and burgages identified for 1619 and earlier (line of Town Wall in bold)

The burgages in Galdeford have considerable variety. On the north-west side of Upper Galdeford are very large burgages, seven of which are 17 perches long or more. It is tempting to see these as an early continuation of the series on the north side of the High Street market place, but such a view is contrary to all that has been postulated about the plan units on the north-south routeway. The south-east side of Upper Galdeford appears to be a secondary development, meshed in with the fine series of burgages on the north side of Lower Galdeford, where 13 plots between F76 and F83 (now Nos. 4-8 and 47) have uniform widths of 2 perches, some of which have been shortened by probably later plots abutting Upper Galdeford. The south side of Lower Galdeford, in contrast, has generally narrower plots, some of which are lamellate in shape, perhaps reflecting earlier strip cultivation. To the east, plots may have been merged together to form enclosed fields, while on the south side nine large burgages reaching to the parish boundary at Weeping Cross Lane, and probably still unoccupied, were granted by the Lord of Ludlow to the Austin Friars in 1254.[82]

Linney is another area neglected by previous writers. The part of Linney immediately outside the town wall, now known as Upper Linney, was perhaps the oldest part of this section of the town, for it was known as 'old Linney' in 15th-century deeds.[83] The steeply sloping street runs outside the town ditch and its course clearly relates to the defences. The rest of Linney, which covers about 40 acres, has modern boundaries which still reflect a rectilinear grid. The area was divided into three series of burgages, each 16 or 17 perches long and 4 perches wide. In the east, there are series either side of the road called 'Linney', which historically was called 'Broad Linney'.[84] The properties in the more easterly of these blocks do not synchronise with those in Corve Street, which suggests that Linney developed later. The third series lies immediately west, east of the track formerly called Green Linney, which in 1884 was the Municipal Boundary, and is now an access track to and along the side of the Rugby Football Ground. The area further west was part of Stanton Lacy parish and the greater part of it was occupied by Castle Meadow, which remained demesne land held with the castle. Nevertheless, the northern part of this meadow was burgaged, as shown by 14th-century title deeds, when it was acquired by the Palmers' Guild.[85] There have been many amalgamations in the Linney area but F269 (Linney Fields), on the west side of the road now called Linney (formerly Broad Linney), exactly 66 feet wide, is a surviving original burgage.

Though many late 13th century documents relate to Linney, there is no firm dating evidence, but some resemblances can be noted to the Leaze at Wimbourne in Dorset.[86] Here,

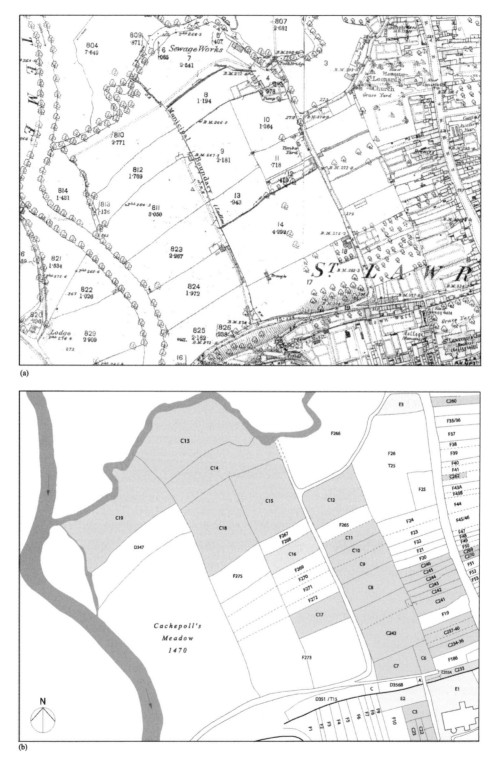

Fig. 24. Linney: OS map extract and burgages identified for 1619 or earlier

'a deserted quarter of the town' was excavated from 1961 to 1966. A large field had 'a long main street longer than 600 feet', with two parallel back lanes. The rectilinear arrangement has similarities with Linney, so it useful to observe that the archaeologists assigned a 12th century date to the earliest artefacts found.

Burgages outside what became the Borough boundary

As well as the developments in the western part of Green Linney, noted above, there was a more spectacular development north-east of Ludlow, on the heart-shaped land between Corve Street, New Road and Gravel Hill/Upper Galdeford, historically part of Stanton Lacy parish. As shown in Fig. 25, the 1849 Stanton Lacy tithe map gives a hint of a rectilinear pattern, with a footpath providing a right of way behind a series of rectangular plots of various sizes. Fig. 25C shows that several of these enclosures were in common ownership with burgages on the east side of Corve Street, some of them used in the 16th century as tenters' yards.[87] The 19th-century right of way was then 'the cross lane behind the yards'. Fig. 25C picks up the strip pattern suggested by these plots and suggests how it might be extended further east, where 'the Rector's Piece' and other properties continue the rectilinear framework.

No such pattern occurred in the north-east, but here there is documentary evidence of burgages. Hill Close is the only land in this part of Ludlow to have been owned by St John's Hospital. In the 14th century part of this area was still burgaged, for before her death in 1355 Joan Mortimer, Countess of March, made a grant to the Hospital of 'four acres of land in Ludlow by our gravel-pit of Sandeputtes, and nine shillings annually from the nine burgages adjacent to the four acres'.[88] Confirmation of burgaging over a wider area than this comes from the accounts of the Lord's bailiff, which survive for 1368 and 1420. The 1368 accounts, compiled a few years after the Mortimer grant, include 103s 6d for '103 and a half burgages from the demesne of the lord at Sandeputtes'.[89] By 1423 the same figure was given, but the term 'chief rents' had replaced 'burgages', implying that the latter were no longer recognisable individually but had been amalgamated into large units.

Probable size of the burgaged area

Unless listed in a single survey, burgage totals must be calculated cautiously. Nevertheless, with over 500 burgages within the borough boundary and more than 100 elsewhere, the intended size of Ludlow as a planned town is impressive, as can be seen in Fig. 1 (p.4). It

69

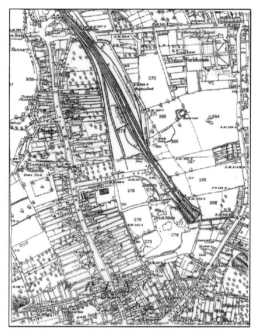

(a) The Corve Street / New Road / Gravel Hill area: 1844 OS extract.

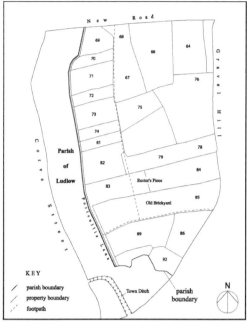

(b) The Corve Street / New Road / Gravel Hill area showing some of the property boundaries and footpaths before the late 19th-century growth of Ludlow (based on Stanton Lacy tythe map).

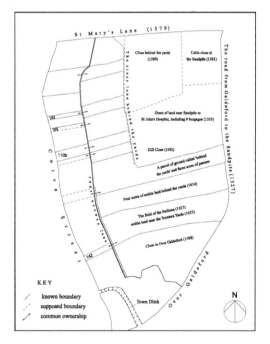

(c) Elements of the historic landscape of the Corve Street / New Road / Gravel Hill area.

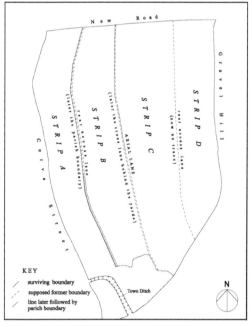

(d) Possible outline initial plan of the Corve Street / New Street / Gravel Hill area, showing the four strips in which burgages might have been arranged.

Fig. 25. Maps to illustrate burgaging between Corve Street, Gravel Hill and New Road

is likely, however, that not all the burgaged areas were for settlement, and both Linney and the north-eastern unit had economic functions from the outset, as suggested by some of the descriptions used.

Because the size of burgages varied, comparison with other new towns on the basis of plot numbers alone can be misleading. It is useful, nevertheless, to compare the Ludlow total of 600 plus with the list of 48 Welsh boroughs provided by Beresford, in which the nearest in size to Ludlow was Cardiff, with 421 burgages. By its area, too, the new town was impressive. The area that became the parish and the borough was 172 acres, but of that Linney accounted for 45 acres, leaving 127 acres for the built up town. This figure is remarkably similar to the 120 acres set aside for 'the fully developed urban area' at the ambitious new town of Salisbury in 1219, though the total area at Salisbury was 260 acres, the cathedral close and the low lying marshy ground known as Burmore accounting for the remaining acreage.

Postscript: the Town Defences

The defensive system for Dinham, linked to the walls of the castle, dates from the 11th or 12th centuries and has been analysed above.[90] It is useful here to offer some reflections on the rest of the walled circuit which, though 13th-century in date, does have implications for the early plan.

Train, cited above,[91] showed conclusively that the stone walls, ditches and gates, in their late medieval form, were built from 1260, financed by a series of murage grants. In several parts of the town, map analysis suggests that the wall and ditch were superimposed on an earlier street layout, causing distortion and dislocation of plots. South of the town, street shapes, continuities of property lines and the size of property blocks all provide evidence of such a process. Lower Mill Street is narrower below the gate than above due to documented encroachment on the east side, but Lower Broad Street extends exactly the sides of the upper part of the street. A field boundary continues the line of Raven Lane beyond the town wall, and excavation in 1992 revealed the stone foundations of buildings which probably abutted to a truncated street.[92] Further east the equivalent street, St John's Lane, survives south of the walls, but its former course can be detected in property boundaries north of Brand Lane. Further evidence comes from the dimensions of the property blocks on either side of Raven Lane, those north of Bell Lane being 4 perches longer than those to the south, suggesting that the latter may have been truncated when the defences were built. On the east side of the town

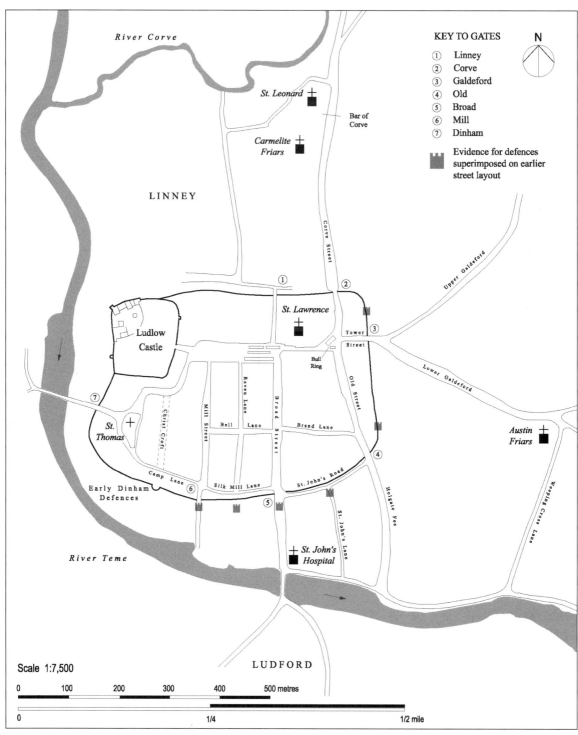

Fig. 26. Map of the town defences (after Train, 1999),
with annotations to illustrate the argument presented in the text

the evidence from map analysis is different but no less persuasive. The four large plots east of Holdgate Fee have features which suggest they were in line with the well preserved burgage pattern on the east side of Corve Street, but the intervening plots show evidence of truncation when the defences were built. It is tempting to postulate that the burgages east of Old Street once extended into Lower Galdeford, some of them terminating at the long, slightly curved plot behind Nos. 105-08 (C92), while others were overlain by the shorter burgages to the west of that property. North of Tower Street, also, the burgages on the east side of the Bull Ring might have extended further east, leaving room for a new, unusually large burgage beyond what became the town ditch.

If these places of supposed superimposition of the walls on an earlier plan are mapped, as on Fig. 26, the result is a massive L-shape, reaching from what became Corve Gate to the lower end of Christ Croft. This is in contrast to the rest of the perimeter, which had the castle and the postulated Dinham defences to the west and south-west, and a natural line of defence in the north, along the edge of the High Street tract, including the churchyard.

It is a possibility – and the idea is put forward tentatively – that this dichotomy provides an answer to the difficulties expressed by Train with regard to the Patent Roll entry for 17th December, 1233, that 'The men of Ludlow have letters for the enclosure of their town'. As shown by Train, this is a one-off grant, made to 'the men of Ludlow', not to their lord. It was a contrast to the series of murage grants made from 1260 to Geoffrey Geneville and his successors as Lords of Ludlow 'to raise money by taxes to enclose the town'. The 1233 grant was made by Henry III at Ledbury, during his passage through the Welsh border at a time of military difficulty, caused by the belligerence of Prince Llywelyn and his followers. Insurgences had occurred since 1218 and earlier, but the autumn of 1233 saw another outbreak of violence, initially in the southern Marches, but threatening to spread north, as indeed occurred the following January when Llywelyn and others 'devastated the border far and wide, making their power felt as far as Shrewsbury'.

It is suggested here that the 1233 grant was not to allow the building of stone walls, as occurred from 1260 onwards, but to allow the men of Ludlow themselves, not their lord, to provide makeshift defences on their own initiative, along the edges of the town not previously defended, i.e. the L-shaped perimeter marked on Fig. 26. The defences were probably an earth rampart with a ditch in front, and perhaps palisades above, of a kind that was relatively cheap to provide, and which could be erected speedily to meet the immediate threat of Welsh spoliation. It was, it is argued, an emergency measure to meet an emergency situation.

Such defences would have entailed the property adjustments on either side of the proposed wall that have been outlined above. Some properties would have shrunk in size, such as those on the east side of Old Street, while others, as the end of the southern blocks between Broad Street and Mill Street, would have disappeared altogether. A key question here is whether the town's administration was advanced enough to undertake such a task, which would inevitably have involved disputes, agitation and perhaps compulsory acquisitions. The evidence is thin, but Faraday (1991) argued, in his account of 'Government' in 'the early borough', that 'the men of Ludlow' were mentioned in the late 12th century in contexts which emphasised their communal status, beginning with the payment of half a mark in 1169 towards a royal aid.[93] Highly motivated by the prospect of Welsh attacks, it seems at least possible that 'the men of Ludlow' could have achieved the necessary organisational authority. But, as Train shows, it was some 25 years later that the great resources of the lordship, through a series of murage grants, were enlisted for the monumental task of constructing the town's stone walls and gates.[94]

Chapter 6

A suggested model for the origins
and early growth of Ludlow

This chapter aims to establish a tentative model for the origins and early history of Ludlow. It draws on the documentary, cartographic and archaeological evidence already presented and reviewed. Some of the information is precise, but much more is speculative, involving various judgements: about the ways in which plot patterns should be interpreted; about the reliability of chroniclers; and about the motivation of those who held the lordship of Ludlow. Where possible such judgements have been made within the context of contemporary events and in the light of what modern scholarship has revealed about Norman towns.

It was shown in chapter 3 that elements of the man-made landscape were in place from an early date, especially the north-south trackway through the town and the Bronze Age tumulus on part of what later became the churchyard.[1] The tumulus may have been used for the burial of Irish saints in the 6th century, but this is uncertain, though there is known to have been Christian activity in the Ludlow area from the 7th century.[2] Place name evidence suggests some economic activity and perhaps small settlements on the site before the Norman conquest. It is possible, as suggested above[3], that the prefix 'lud' in the place name Ludlow is the name of a Saxon infidel called Luda, but on balance it is more likely that the meaning is topographical, relating to the 'loud waters' of the turbulent River Teme.[4]

The weight of recent scholarship favours Walter de Lacy I as the first builder of Ludlow Castle, perhaps in the 1070s, and there is convincing evidence of a contemporary settlement at Dinham.[5] This was probably protected by a ditch on the eastern side and some other defensive work to the south, along the line later followed by the 13th-century town wall.[6] Though various sources record that the name of this settlement was Dinan, the name of a

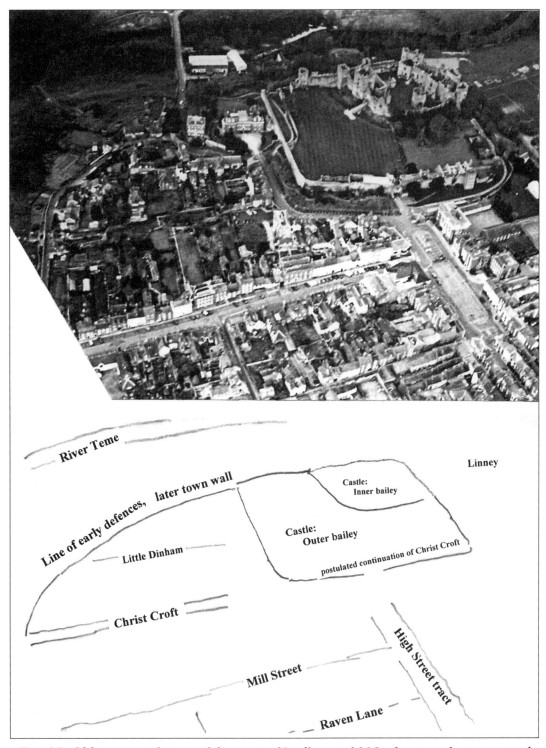

Fig. 27. Oblique aerial view of the west of Ludlow in 2005, showing the integrated castle/Dinham plan unit, with parts of other units

later lord of Ludlow, it is more likely that the word used was Dinham, the elements of which are older.[7] The population of this settlement, like those of other known hamlets, must have been included with that of Stanton (Lacy) in the Domesday Survey of 1085, details of which were considered in chapter 4.[8] That chapter reviews the suggestion that there was another early settlement along the line of what was later called Old Street, with its own market place east of what became the churchyard.[9] Plan analysis, discussed in chapter 5, provides some support for this speculation, but the evidence is not conclusive, and the number of outlying settlements that can be embraced by the estimated population of Domesday Stanton – between 600 and 700 – is not unlimited.[10]

A dramatic expansion of the first settlement on the site of Ludlow is most likely to have occurred after 1115, when the lordship was secured by Payn fitzJohn (d.1137), an 'upwardly mobile' Norman administrator who married the heiress of Hugh de Lacy II and became Sheriff of both Shropshire and Herefordshire.[11] The High Street tract, with its 'generously proportioned market place' and large burgages, is most likely to have been laid out at Payn fitzJohn's bidding. A case can be made, also, that bilateral burgaging occurred at this time along the ancient north-south routeway, absorbing any earlier settlement to create what became Old Street, the Bull Ring and Corve Street.[12] These two units – the High Street tract and the line of Old Street-Bull Ring-Corve Street – both have 'deep' burgages, providing what Conzen (1988) called their 'period index' and supporting the view that they were both laid out in the 1115-1137 period.[13] The 'new town' that resulted was essentially T-shaped, comparable in layout to the Norman town at Farnham, though with the settlement at Dinham and its defences adjoining the castle.[14] Different burgage widths indicate that Corve Street grew in phases but the most northerly burgages on the western side, the 12 that became part of Dinmore Fee, were there before 1186, a date clearly defined in the Hundred Rolls.[15]

According to a chronicler writing before 1154, the castle may have been called '*Lodelowe*' by 1138 and a later chronicler applied this name to the town also.[16] Both castle and town became embroiled in the civil war between Stephen and Matilda, the former giving the castle to his supporter Joce de Dinan. Joce is prominently featured in the Fitzwarine Romance, but as this is a narrative written a century and a half later, his role may be exaggerated. Joce is credited in the Romance with building 'a bridge of stone and lime' across the River Teme, but the authenticity of this cannot be checked, though there is some supporting architectural evidence at Ludford bridge.[17] The uncertainties of civil war between 1139 and 1153 were not a propitious time for town development and there is no evidence, apart from the Romance, that Ludlow expanded further at this time. In the closing years of the period the castle reverted to Gilbert de Lacy, but though he was probably responsible for building the chapel of St Mary Magdalene in the castle, there are no indications that he promoted growth of the town.[18]

Gilbert's son Hugh de Lacy II, however, was a known developer of towns, as well as being a baron of burning ambition, who supported Henry II at the invasion of Ireland in 1171, eventually holding high office in that country.[19] It seems almost certain that he was responsible for the 'middle and southern plan unit', with its sophisticated planning based on mathematical principles available to the surveyors of towns through such works as the translation of Euclid by Adelard of Bath, circulating from about 1140.[20] Burgages were generally shorter than those in the two plan units considered above, which was, in part perhaps, a deliberate policy to increase housing density as the population of the new town increased.[21] One of the main thoroughfares, Broad Street, continued the line of Ludford Bridge, which, if not built by Joce de Dinan, must date from soon afterwards.

The core of the town was now in place, with four distinctive plan units: Dinham, here attributed to Walter de Lacy I in the 1070s; the High Street tract and the bilateral development of Old Street/Bull Ring/Corve Street, both here attributed to Payn fitzJohn in the two decades after 1115; and the sophisticated 'middle and southern plan' unit, attributed to Hugh de Lacy II, perhaps before his involvement in Ireland from 1171. To this core, other accretions were added. The most enigmatic are those in Upper and Lower Galdeford, where a number of different burgage patterns can be detected, though there was considerable adjustment to the construction of the town defences in the 13th century. Very different kinds of accretion, with a different functional purpose, occurred on either side of the Corve Street. burgages. These were large rectilinear plots, usually 4 perches wide, that were arranged in parallel north and south series. To the west these formed Broad Linney and Green Linney on the level alluvial plain of the Rivers Teme and Corve.[22] To the east, the pattern is similar, though less well preserved, and rises onto the gravel terraces at what is now Gravel Hill.[23]

By 1200 or a little earlier, it is contended, the new town of Ludlow was fully grown, though important amendments to the plan were made in the 13th century. Documentary records of the years after 1165, considered in chapter 4, though still sparse, reveal a town with considerable economic activity, and with some vestiges of self government.[24] Most significantly, the town had a church independent of the mother parish of Stanton, with its own

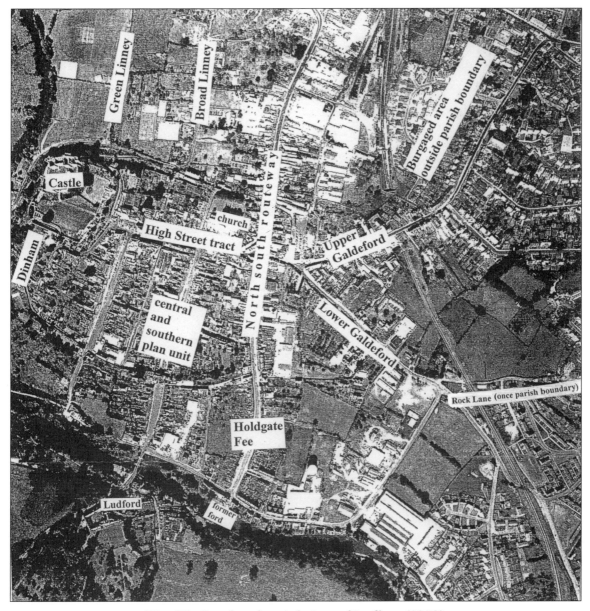

*Fig. 28. Overhead aerial view of Ludlow (1972),
showing the greater part of the historic town, with some adjoining fields and suburbs*

vicar deputising for an absentee rector, and had almost certainly assumed the parish boundary that was to survive for many centuries.[25] This is a key point in the chronology suggested here, which has not been made by any other writer. The rebuilding of the church from 1199 suggests an enlarged and thriving town, while the legend of the Irish saints, whatever its authenticity, can be seen as an attempt to give the town status and authority.[26]

The market colonisation and encroachment of the High Street market place almost certainly began in the 12th century, but continued after 1200, encouraging the sale of livestock to take place also in neighbouring streets, some of which may have been shaped for this function.[27] Groups of burgages were made available for religious institutions, as at St John's Hospital at the bottom of Lower Broad Street and at the Austin Friary at the south-east end of Lower Galdeford, the latter causing the diversion of Friars' Walk, which had previously followed the entrenched parish boundary that formerly divided Stanton and Ludford.[28]

The most dramatic amendments were those involving the town defences. It has been suggested that the construction of preliminary defences on the eastern and southern side of

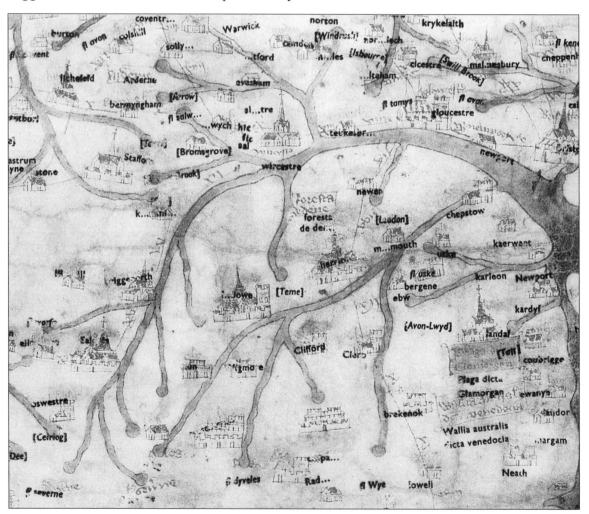

Fig. 29. Ludlow in its regional setting, as portrayed on the Gough map. North is to the left, with the Bristol Channel prominently shown

the town caused considerable dislocation of earlier burgage patterns in 1233 and afterwards.[29] This was followed by the building of stone walls and gates around the central part of the town from 1260. This process created suburbs north, east and south of the town, of which the largest was that of Corve Street to the north, an impressive urban feature comparable to Wigford at Lincoln or Fore Street at Totnes.[30]

No visual image of 13th-century Ludlow exists, in fact the earliest pictorial representation of any kind is that of the Gough map of Great Britain, which dates from the mid-14th century.[31] The image is reproduced opposite, seen within its regional setting. It shows a town with the tall church tower, a defensive wall with flanking towers, a more substantial tower which may represent the castle, and a cluster of red roofs, perhaps made of tiles. Clearly, this is symbolic rather than pictorial, but comparison with the way that neighbouring settlements are represented supports the documentary evidence and the plan analysis to show that medieval Ludlow was a substantial town with an image comparable in size to those used for the county towns of Shrewsbury and Hereford.

To a high degree the plan of the Norman founders survives to this day: the essentials of their vision are intact, though the town that resulted seems to have been smaller than the very large urban development which was intended.[32] Using documentary, cartographic and archaeological evidence, this publication has suggested a sequence of events which seems to the author the most plausible in the context of the limited knowledge we have. It is offered as a stimulant to further debate and reinterpretation; and for refinement as further evidence comes to light.

Appendix

Alleged 6th-century burial of Irish saints, as recorded by medieval chroniclers

Translated from the Latin by Michael Faraday

Leland (Latin text in Wright, 1852, p. 14)

In 1199 it happened in a certain district in England, that is, in the province of Shrewsbury, in a neighbourhood which is called Ludlow, that the inhabitants of the same town decided to build its church longer because it was too short to contain the people belonging to it within it. On which account it was necessary to level the earth of a great mound of earth to the west of the church to which the wall of the same ought to be extended. While they levelled the aforesaid hill by digging they came across three stone tombs and the dead bodies of saints, which when they appeared they restored the remains of the three saints. Set out in writing on one wooden plaque, of which the first was wrapped in wax inside and outside in lead, were these words in English:

Here lie the blessed relics of St Fercher the father of Brendan, understood to be Irish saints, covered in earth and beautiful stone. Also the holy Corona, mother of the aforesaid Brendan, aunt of Columkill, the elect of God, St. Cochel, the aunt of Columkill brother of the same saints. There have passed fifteen years after the death of the infidel Luda since the remains of the British saints came here.

Of which remains the clerks of the same church lifting from the soil and placed them together in a wooden vault in the church making a fitting reliquary on 3 Ides of April [= 11 April]. So far as the Lord deigns to bring about any miracles by their merits and intercessions, to him be praise, honour and glory for ever. Amen.

Llandaff

(transcribed by Michael Faraday)

MCC: Hoc tempore campanile de Ludelowe cum corpore ecclesie ex fundamento constructus est in quo fundamento iii idus Aprilus tria mausincula lapidem inventa sunt et in eis sanctorum reliquie hoc scripto in cedula que prius intersecus cera exterius vero plumbo fuerat involuta hiis verbis anglice sunt detecte:

Hic requiescunt sanctus Ferchere pater Brendani beata pignora Sancti scilicet herbernenses lapide solo inclusi sancta quoque Ona mater prelibati Brendani matertera vicelicet Columkille electe Dei sanctus etiam Cochel germanus eiusdem hic nempe quindenis dequerunt annis dum sanctorum Britannie adierunt patertinia post obitum Lude increduli.

1200: At this time the Ludlow tower with the body of the church was built from its foundations in which foundations on 3 Ides of April three stone coffins were found and in them the remains of saints. In writing on a plaque which before it was wrapped inside in wax, and outside in lead, were revealed these words in English:

Here lie St. Ferchere father of Brendan the blessed relics of the Irish saints covered in earth and stone; Ona mother of the aforementioned Brendan aunt of Columkill the elect of God, St. Cochel brother of the same. There passed 15 years after the death of the infidel Luda since the relics of the British saints came here.

Abbreviations and Select Bibliography

Abbreviations

BL:	British Library
LB:	Ludlow Borough
SA:	Shropshire Archives
S.Arch.	Shropshire Archaeology
VCH:	Victoria County History

Select bibliography

Bateson, M., 1900, 'The Laws of Breteuil', *English Historical Review*, 5, pp.73-78

Beresford, M., 1988, *New Towns of the Middle Ages*, 2nd ed. (Gloucester)

Conzen, M.R.G., 1968, 'The Use of Town Plans in the Study of Urban History', in Dyos, H.J. (ed.), *The Study of Urban History* (London), pp.113-130

Conzen, M.R.G., 1988, 'Morphogenesis, Morphological Regions and Secular Human Agency in the Historic Townscape, as Exemplified by Ludlow', in Denecke, D. and Shaw, G. (eds.), *Urban Historical Geography*: *Recent Progress in Britain and Germany,* (Cambridge), pp.253-72

Coplestone-Crow, B., 1995, 'Payn FitzJohn and Ludlow Castle', *TSAS*, 78, pp.171-83

Coplestone-Crow, B., 2000, 'From Foundation to Anarchy', in Shoesmith, R. and Johnson, A., (eds.), *Ludlow Castle, Its History and Buildings* (Logaston), pp.31-34

Dalwood, H. et al., 1996, *Archaeological Assessment of Ludlow, Shropshire*, Shropshire County Council and Worcester County Council

Eyton, R.W., 1853-60, *The Antiquities of Shropshire* (London), 12 vols.

Faraday, M.A., 1991, *Ludlow 1085-1660*: *A Social, Economic and Political History* (Chichester)

Gelling, M., 1984, *Place Names in the Landscape* (London)

Gelling, M., 1990, *The Place Names of Shropshire* (English Place Name Society, Nottingham)

Gelling, M., 1992, *The West Midlands in the Early Middle Ages* (Leicester)

Hathaway, E.J., Ricketts, P.T., Robson, C.A., and Wiltshire, A.D., *Fouke Fitzwarin* (Anglo-Norman texts, 1975)

Hindle, B.P., 1981, *The Study of Medieval Town Plans with special reference to Shropshire*, University of Salford Department of Geography, Discussion Paper 14

Hindle, B.P., 1990, *Medieval Town Plans*, Shire Archaeology (Princes Risborough)

Hooke, D., 1985, *The Anglo-Saxon landscape: The Kingdom of the Hwicce* (Manchester)

Lilley, K.D., 1997, 'Colonialism and urbanism in high medieval Europe, identifying morphologies of urban change', in De Boe, G. and Verhaeghe, F. (eds.), *Urbanism in Medieval Europe* (IAP Rapporten, Zellik), pp.189-204

Lilley, K.D., 1998, 'Taking measure across the medieval landscape: aspects of urban design before the Renaissance', *Urban Morphology*, 2(2), pp.82-92

Lloyd, D.J. and Klein, P., 1984, *Ludlow: A Historic Town in Words and Pictures* (Chichester)

Lloyd, D.J., 2005, 'Property, ownership and improvement in Ludlow, a fashionable country town, 1660 to 1848', unpublished PhD thesis, University of Wolverhampton

Renn, D., 1987, 'Castel de Dynan: the first phase of Ludlow', in Kenyon, J.R. and Avent, R. (eds.), *Castles in Wales and the Marches: Essays in Honour of D.J. Cathcart King* (Cardiff)

St John Hope, W.H., 1909A, 'The Castle of Ludlow', *Archaeologia*, 61 (1909), pp. 257-358

St John Hope, W.H., 1909B, 'The Ancient Topography of the Town of Ludlow', *Archaeologia*, 61, pp.383-88

Shoesmith, R. and Johnson, A., 2000, *Ludlow Castle, Its History and Buildings* (Logaston)

Slater, T., 1990, 'English medieval new towns with composite plans: evidence from the Midlands', in Slater, T. (ed.), *The Built Form of Western Cities* (Leicester), pp.60-82

Thorn, F. and C., 1986, *Domesday Book* (ed. Morris, G.), *25, Shropshire* (Chichester)

Train, C., 1999, *The Walls and Gates of Ludlow* (Ludlow Research Papers, New Series, No.1)

Wightman, W.E., 1966, *The Lacy Family in England and Normandy, 1066-1194*, (Oxford)

Wright, T., 1852, *History of Ludlow* (Ludlow)

Endnotes

Chapter 1

1. Hey, D., *The Oxford Guide to Family History* (Oxford, 1993), p.2.
2. Borsay, P., *The Image of Georgian Bath, 1700-2000, Towns, Heritage and History* (Oxford, 2000), pp.49-50.
3. Strawthorn, J., *Royal Burgh and County Town* (Edinburgh, 1980), p.2.
4. Lamplugh, L., *Barnstaple, Town on the Taw* (Chichester, 1983), p.2.
5. Beraman, R. (ed.), *The History of an English Borough: Stratford-upon-Avon, 1196-1996* (Stroud, 1997), p.vii.
6. In 2001, the population was 9, 944, *Census: Population* (Office of National Statistics), Table CAS 002.
7. Beresford, 1988, p.481.
8. Slater, 1990, p.78.
9. Palliser, D. M., 'The origins of British towns', *The Cambridge Urban History of Britain*, Vol. I (2000), p.19.
10. Shoesmith, R., *Hereford: History and Guide* (Stroud, 1992), p.8.
11. Reynolds, S., *An Introduction to the History of English Medieval Towns* (Oxford, 1977), p.35.
12. Tait, J., 'Introduction to Shropshire Domesday', in Page, W., *VCH, Shropshire*, I (London, 1908), pp.279-308.
13. Stamper, P., 'Domesday Book to 1300: Marketing', in *VCH, Shropshire*, IV (London, 1989), p.66.
14. Ibid, p.68.
15. Faraday, 1991, p.157.
16. Beresford, 1988, pp.55-97.
17. Ibid, pp.479-82; Croom, J., 'The Topographical Analysis of Medieval Town Plans: The Examples of Much Wenlock and Bridgnorth', *Midland History*, Vol. XVII (1992), p.31.
18. Watkins-Pritchard, W. *The Shropshire Hearth-Tax Roll of 1672* (Shropshire Archaeological and Parish Register Society), 1949.
19. *VCH, Shropshire*, II, p.224; Lloyd, D., Payne, R., Train, C. and Williams, D., *Victorian Ludlow* (Bucknell, 2004).
20. Braithwaite, L. *The Historic Towns of Britain* (London, 1981), p.120.
21. *VCH, Shropshire*, II, p.224.
22. Kelly, *Directory of Shropshire* (London, 1900), p.126.
23. Dalwood, 1996, p.18.

Chapter 2

1. Camden, W., *Britannia: A Chorographical description of the flourishing Kingdoms of England, Scotland and Ireland from the earliest antiquity* (London, 1587), p.386.
2. Eyton, R.W., *Antiquities of Shropshire*, vol. 5 (1861), p.234.
3. Train, 1999, pp.20-25.
4. Camden, *Britannia*, p.386; Skeel, C.A.J., *The Council in the Marches of Wales* (London, 1904), pp.20, 30, 49.
5. Wharton, T., *Poems upon Several Occasions by John Milton* (London, 1785), p.112.
6. Wright, 1852, p.34.
7. Ibid, pp.54-60.
8. Hathaway et al, 1975.
9. Palmer, S., *The Reign of King John* (London, 1949), p.127; Hathaway et.al., p.xxxvi.
10. Cited in Lloyd and Klein, 1984, p.16.
11. Wright, 1852, p.15.

12. Gelling, 1990, p.186.
13. Rolls series, e.g. 75, Arnold, T., *Henrici Archdiacon Huntendubensis Historica Anglloram*, (London, 1879); Pipe Roll Society volumes, *Henry II* and *Richard I* (London, 1905-26).
14. St John Hope, 1909A, p.324.
15. St John Hope, 1909B.
16. Ibid, p.384.
17. Ibid, p.387.
18. Ibid, p.384.
19. Ibid, pp.384-85.
20. St John Hope, 1909A, p.324.
21. Butler, L., 'The evolution of towns after 1066', in 'The plans and topography of medieval towns in England and Wales', in Barley, M.W., *Council of British Archaeology Report*, 14, p.38.
22. Beresford, 1988.
23. Ibid, pp.65-68.
24. Ibid, p.481-82.
25. The rental is now SA, Lb, 4/2/7.
26. Conzen, *Alnwick, Northumberland, A Study in town Plan Analysis*, Institute of British Geographers, 27 (London, 1960).
27. Conzen, 1968
28. Dyos, H.J. (ed.), *The Study of Urban History* (London, 1968).
29. Conzen, *Alnwick*, pp.4-5.
30. Conzen, 1968, p.117.
31. Ibid, pp.122-124.
32. Ibid, pp.124-126.
33. Ludlow W.E.A. Historical Research Group, Publication No.1, *A Ludlow Burgage Rental of 1619*, transcribed and edited by E.L. Morley, 1965.
34. File in possession of the author.
35. Beresford, 1988, p.481. The 1482 rental is now numbered SA, LB, 4/2/7.
36. Rowley, T., *The Shropshire Landscape*, The Making of the English Landscape series (London, 1972), pp.182-86, and plate 24 (facing p.169).
37. Speight, M.E. and Lloyd, D.J., *Ludlow Houses and their Residents*, Ludlow Research Paper No.1 (Ludlow, 1977).
38. e.g. Lloyd, D. and Moran, M., *The Corner Shop*, Ludlow Research Paper No.2 (Ludlow, 1978), p.25.
39. Platt, C., *The English Medieval Town* (London, 1976), p.35.
40. Hindle, 1981, pp.29/30, Fig.8 (endpaper).
41. Conzen, 1988, p.264.
42. Ibid, p.266.
43. Ibid, pp.266-68. However, the writer cannot accept Conzen's thinking in this paper that the Broad Street-Mill Street unit, with its distinctive access lane between, was a mid 13th-century development, influenced by trading in wine with Gascony.
44. Slater, *The analysis of burgages in medieval towns*, Dept. of Geography, University of Birmingham, Working Paper 41, 1981.
45. Slater, 1990, pp.74-77.
46. Ibid, pp.77-78.
47. Hindle, 1990, p.60.
48. Renn, 1987, p.58.
49. Coplestone-Crow, 2000, pp.21-22.
50. Train, 1999, pp.20-25.
51. Gelling, 1990.
52. Ekwall, E., *The Concise Oxford Dictionary of English Place-Names* (4th ed., Oxford, 1970), pp.145, 213.
53. Copleston-Crow, 2000, p.27.
54. Lloyd and Klein, 1984, p.16.
55. Faraday, 1991, pp.1-2.
56. Lilley, 1997, p.192.
57. Ibid, p.195.
58. Ibid, p.198.
59. Lilley, 1998.
60. Notes on file.
61. Dalwood, 1996, p.19.
62. Ibid, pp.21-22.
63. Shoesmith, 2000, p.9; Houghton, A.W.J., 'A Roman Road from Ashton, North Herefordshire, to Marshbrook, Salop', *T.S.A.S.*, lvii (1961), pp.185-190.

64. Shoesmith, 2000, p.11-12.
65. Ibid. p.13.
66. Ibid, pp.13-14.
67. Botfield, B., 'On the discovery of the remains of the Priory of Austin Friars at Ludlow', *Archaeologia*, xxxix (1862), p.183.
68. St John Hope, 1909A, 1909B.
69. Klein, P. and Roe, A., 1987, pp.46-47.
70. Dalwood, 1996, end paper.
71. S.Arch., 3841.
72. S.Arch., 3772.
73. S.Arch., 6110.
74. Marches Archaeology, Lyonshall, Herefordshire, series 308.
75. Inf. ex. D.Garner, Gifford and Partners Ltd., Chester.
76. Hughes, E.H., Ludlow College Sports Hall, Archaeological Evaluation, S. Arch., 6112.
77. S.Arch., 6115.
78. Marches Archaeology, Lyonshall, series 308.
79. Train, 1999, p.33.
80. Ludlow Museum 4206, notes by Dr Paul Stamper.

Chapter 3

1. Gelling, 1990, p.186. There is a River Loud in east Lancashire.
2. Ibid.
3. Earp, J.R. and Haines, B.A., *British Regional Geology: The Welsh Borderland*, 3rd ed. (1971).
4. Conzen, 1968, p.125.
5. Account of Richard Pauntley, 1368, SA, LB, box 417.
6. Churchyard, Thomas, *The Worthiness of Wales*: *A Poem* (London, 1587, reprinted by Thomas Evans, London, 1776.
7. Conzen, 1966, p.126.
8. Houghton, A.W.J., 'A Roman road from Ashton, north Herefordshire, to Marshbrook, Salop', *T.S.A.S.*, lviii (1964) p.185; Shoesmith, R., 'The Town of Ludlow', in Shoesmith, R. and Johnson, A., *Ludlow Castle: Its History and Buildings* (Logaston, 2000), pp.5-9.
9. Chitty, L., 'The Clun-Clee Ridgeway: A prehistoric track across south Shropshire'. In Foster, I. and Alcock, I., *Culture and Environment* (PLACE, 1963).
10. I am indebted for this phrase to my LHRG colleague Dr Margaret Clark.
11. Eyton, 1854, p.292.
12. Faraday, p.53.
13. Wright, 1852, p.14.
14. BL: Cotton Nero, A.iv, *Cronica Landavenses*, Ff.48v.
15. *Illustrated Handbook to Ludlow* (Ludlow, 1878), p.2.
16. Foster, R.F., *The Oxford Illustrated History of Ireland* (Oxford, 1991), p.10.
17. Gelling, M., 1992, pp.94, 97.
18. Faraday, 1991, p.53.
19. Ekwall, E., *The Concise Oxford Dictionary of English Place-Names* (Oxford, 4th ed., 1960); Gelling, 1990, p.186.
20. Stanford, S., *The Archaeology of the Welsh Marches* (London, 1980), pp.67-68.
21. Ekwall, op. cit., p.242.
22. Hooke, D., *The Anglo-Saxon landscape: the kingdom of the Hwice* (Manchester, 1985), pp.41-43.
23. Ekwall, op. cit., p.307.
24. Ibid.
25. See p.19.
26. Ludlow Historical Research Group, day conference, 1999; Gelling, *1992,* p.125; Ackroyd, P*., London the Biography*, 2001, p.11.
27. See fn.12 and 13.
28. Keynes, S., 'Diocese and Cathedral before 1056', in Aylmer, G. and Tiller, J., *Hereford Cathedral*: *A History* (London, 2000), p.3.
29. Steenton, F., *Anglo-Saxon England* (Oxford, 2nd ed., 1947), p.46.
30. Hooke, 1985, p.7.
31. Ibid.

32. Keynes, op.cit.

33. Ibid.

34. Klein, P., *A Guide to St Peter's Church, Stanton Lacy* (Stanton Lacy, 1983), p.2.

35. Blair, J., 'The Anglo-Saxon Church in Herefordshire: Four Themes', in Malpas, A., et.al, *The Early Church in Herefordshire: Proceedings of a Conference held in Leominster*, June 2000 (Leominster, 2001), p.5.

36. Lloyd, D. and Klein, P., *Ludlow: A Historic Town in Words and Pictures* (Chichester, 1984), p.12.

37. Blair, op. cit., p.3.

38. Blair, op. cit., p.1.

39. Newman, J. and Pevsner, N., *The Buildings of England: Shropshire*, 2006 ed., p.600.

40. Jones, A, *A Thousand Years of the English Parish* (Moreton in Marsh, 2000), p.125.

41. Evans, C., *A Map of the Borough of Ludlow*, 1832.

42. Ibid.

43. *Cal. Patent Rolls*, 1281-92, p.116.

44. Faraday, 1991, p.15; Thorn, 1986, pp.4, 21, 16.

45. See pp.7-8.

46. Faraday, 1991, p.1.

47. Gelling, 1984, p.73.

48. Ibid, pp.34-36.

49. I owe this last paragraph to Dr Margaret Clark.

Chapter 4

1. Coplestone-Crow, 2000, p.21.

2. Wightman, 1966, end paper, genealogical table.

3. Faraday, 1991, pp.3-5.

4. Based on the observations and research of Joanne Lindsay; see also pp.45-46.

5. Information from the then Mayor of Lassy and other local residents.

6. Copleston-Crow, 2000, p.22.

7. St John Hope, 1909A, p.324.

8. Renn, 'The Norman Military Works', in Shoesmith, R. and Johnson, A., 2000, p.130.

9. Newman, J., *Shropshire*, Buildings of England series (2nd ed., Harmondsworth, 2006), p.362.

10. I am indebted for information and advice on this section to the Domesday scholar, Dr Sally P.J. Harvey, now Lady Fielding, who lives at Elton, near Ludlow.

11. Wightman, 1966, p.168.

12. Thorn, F. and C., 7/4.

13. Using a multiplier of 5 for all persons listed.

14. Thorn, F. and C., op.cit.

15. Thorn F. and C., 7/4, note; see chapter 3, pp.33-35.

16. Ekwall, E., *The Concise Oxford Dictionary of English Place Names* (Oxford, 4th ed., 1960).

17. Morgan, P., *Domesday Book and the Local Historian* (Historical Association, 1988), p.37.

18. I am indebted to Alan Hurley for the information and arguments used in this paragraph.

19. See p.32.

20. Based on Wightman, 1966, pp.167-175.

21. Wightman., 1966, p.135, fn.

22. Coplestone-Crowe, 1995, p.171; Wightman, 1966, pp.174-75. The rest of this and the next paragraph are from these sources, unless stated otherwise.

23. Fraser, A., *The Lives of the Kings and Queens of England* (2nd ed., London, 1998), p.32.

24. Thorpe, L. (ed.), *Gerald of Wales, The Journey through Wales*, (1978), p.94.

25. Coplestone- Crow, 1995, pp.171-172.

26. See pedigrees above.

27. Ibid, p.171.

28. Beresford, 1988, pp.638, 642.

29. Coplestone-Crow, pp.23-24.

30. Arnold, T. (ed.), *Henrici Archidiacon Huntendunensis Historia Anglorum*, R.S., 75 (London, 1879), pp.261, 265. Coplestone-Crow, B., 1995, pp.180-181.

31. See n.24.

32. *Chronica Monasterii de Melsa*, R.S.43 (1851), p.17.

33. Wightman, 1966, p.141.

34. Coplestone-Crowe (2000), pp.217-218, argues that Dinan married the widow of Payn fitzJohn, but the evidence is not conclusive.

35. Faraday, 1991, p.3.

36. Hathaway, etc., p.36.

37. Lloyd and Klein, 1984, p.17.

38. Lewis, C.P., Lacy, Gilbert de (fl.1133-1163), Oxford Dictionary of National Biography (2000), vol. 32.

39. www.renderplus.com/hartgen/htm/talbot. htm; I am grateful to Joanne Lindsay for pointing out this and other inconsistencies in the published work on Gilbert de Lacy.

40. Flanagan, M.T., 'Hugh de Lacy' (d.1186), *O.D.N.B.* (2004), Vol. 23, pp.184-85.

41. Lilley, 1998, pp.83-84.

42. Ex. Dr Anthony Streeton, Inspector of Ancient Monuments with English Heritage.

43. Renn, D. and Shoesmith, R., 'The Outer Bailey', in Shoesmith and Johnson (eds.), *Ludlow Castle*: *Its History and Buildings* (Almeley, 2000*)*, p.194.

44. St John Hope, 1909A, p.385.

45. PRO, Hundred Rolls, ii, 69.

46. Flanagan, M.T., 'Lacy, Walter de' (d.1241), *D.N.B.*, Vol. 32, pp.201-203.

47. Weyman, H.T., 'Confirmation by Walter de Lacy of the Hospital of St John', *TSAS*, ser.3, vol. iv (1904), p.xviii; ibid, 'A Grant by Walter de Lacy to Ludlow Church', *TSAS*, ser.4, vol. ix (1923), pp.263-267.

48. Bateson, 1900. pp.312-13, Ludlow; this paragraph is based on Bateson's article.

49. Faraday, 1991, p.20.

50. Pipe Roll Society Volumes, *Henry II* and *Richard I* (London, 1905-26).

51. Ibid, *2 Richard I*, p.125.

52. Ibid, *33 Henry II*, p.64.

53. RS 53, *Historical and Municipal Documents of Ireland, 1172-1320*, p.7: Dublin Roll of Burgages for second half of twelfth century; names include John de Ludelowe, Adam tailor of Lodelowe; Robert Summer of Lodelowe.

54. Weyman, H.T., *Ludlow in Bye-Gone Days*, Ludlow, 1913, pp.33-35.

55. Faraday, pp.20-27.

56. Cheney, C.R., *English Bishops' Chantries, 1100-1250* (Manchester, 1950), cited in Lloyd, D.J., 1977, p.176.

57. Ibid.

58. Jones, A., *A Thousand Years of the English Parish* (Moreton-in-Marsh, 2000), p.16.

59. Cheney, C.R., English Bishops' Chantries, 1100-1250 (Manchester, 1950), pp.157-58.

60. Jones, op. cit., p.49.

61. Faraday, 1991, p.157.

62. Thorn, F. and C., 1986, 7, 4.

63. Lloyd and Klein, 1984, pp.16-17.

64. *Pipe Rolls*, 9 Richard I (1197).

65. Faraday, 1991, p.138.

66. PRO, Feet of Fines, CR 25(1)/193/2.

67. PRO, Just.1.732.

Chapter 5

1. See p.13.

2. Slater, 1990, p.61.

3. Conzen, M.R.G., *Alnwick, Northumberland, A Study in Town-Plan Analysis*, The Institute of British Geographers, pub.17 (London, 1960), p.5.

4. Slater, T.T., 'The topography and planning of medieval Lichfield: a critique', *Transactions, South Staffordshire Archaeological and Historical Society*, 16 (1986), pp.11-35, Bond, J., 'Central place and medieval new town: the origins of Thame, Oxfordshire' in Slater, T.R. (ed.), *The Built Form of Western Cities* (Leicester, 1990), pp.83-108.

5. Bateson, 1900, p.73.

6. SA, LB, 4.2/29.

7. SA, LA, 4/2/28.

8. Ludlow Corporation Ledger, in possession of the writer.

9. SA, LB, 4/2/7.

10. SA, LB, 4/2/6.

11. SA, LB, 5/3/62 & 63.
12. Lloyd, 2005, pp.144-150.
13. Slater, 1990, pp.74-77.
14. Lilley, 1997, p.195.
15. See p.38.
16. Train, 1999, p.23.
17. St John Hope, 1909B, p.385.
18. Conference on the origins of Ludlow, 1982.
19. SA, LB, 4/2/29; *Hereford Journal*, 29 July 1779, sale notice of 'two new built freehold houses, fronting the walk in Dinham' (related to Nos. 11 and 12 Dinham).
20. See p.35.
21. Dalwall, 1996, p.7.
22. Renn, 1987, p.58.
23. Train, 1999, pp.24-25.
24. Conzen, 1988, p.263-264.
25. SA, LB, 4/2/6 & 7.
26. Conzen, 1988, p.264.
27. Lilley, 1997, pp.193-195.
28. Weyman, 1913, pp.40-41.
29. Inf. ex. Sir Christopher Davison, 25 October 1999, following visit.
30. Faraday, 1991, p.56.
31. e.g. SA, LB, 4/2/2 (Register of leases), p.119.
32. S. Arch., 00519.
33. See p.8.
34. BL, Chronica Lladavensis, Cotton, Nero A., IV.
35. See p.22.
36. Train, 1999, pp.22-23.
37. Conzen, 1968, p.124.
38. St John Hope, 1909A, p.259.
39. Dymond, D. and Northeast, P., *A History of Suffolk* (Chichester, 1985), p.37.
40. Slater, 1990, p.69.
41. Conzen, 1988, p.265.
42. Aston, M. and Bond, J., *The Landscape of Towns* (Gloucester, 1987), pp.96-97.
43. SA, LA, 5/3/62 & 63.
44. RS, *Hundred Rolls*, 1255, p.68.
45. SA, LA, 5/3/62.
46. S. Arch., 3772.
47. Weyman, 1913, p.47
48. SA, LB, 5/3/63, late 13th century Palmers' Guild rental.
49. Weyman, 1913, pp.35-37.
50. Conzen, 1968, pp.124-25.
51. Hindle, 1981, p.29, fig. 8.
52. Hindle, 1990, p.60; see p.17.
53. Slater, 1990, p.78.
54. Lilley, 1997, p.194; see p.21.
55. Conzen, 1988, p.266.
56. RS, *Hundred Rolls*, 1255, p.68.
57. Slater, 1990, p.78.
58. Weyman, 1913, p.35; Slater, 1990, p.78.
59. St John Hope, 1909A, p.384.
60. Conzen, 1968, p.124.
61. Conzen, 1968, p.126.
62. Conzen, 1968, pp.126-128.
63. Lilley, 1997, pp.194-198.
64. Hughes, E.H., *Ludlow College Sports Hall, Archaeological Evaluation*, 1990.
65. See pp.51-53.
66. St John Hope, 1909B, p.387.
67. St John Hope, 1909B, p.305.
68. SA, LB, 4/2/34.
69. Slater, 1990, p.72; see Fig. 5, p.16.
70. SA, LB, 4/2/7.
71. Slater, 1990, pp.74-77.
72. SA, LB, 4/2/6.
73. PRO, KB, 27/97, Stephen de Butterley v John, son of Robert Hawkins.
74. Slater, 1990, p.76.
75. Lilley, 1998, pp.85-87.
76. See p.54.
77. Slater, 1990, p.70-71.
78. Conzen, 1968, p.125.
79. Hindle, 1961, fig. 8.
80. Lilley, 1998, p.194.
81. e.g., SA, LB, MT 3, 8, 25.
82. Chibnall, M.M., 'The Austin Friars of Ludlow', *VCH Shropshire*, Vol. II, p.20.
83. SA, LB, MT 672.
84. SA, LB, 4/1/6.

85. SA, LB, MT 572, 649, 653.
86. Field, N., 'The Leaze, Wimbourne, an excavation in a deserted quarter of the town', *Proceedings of the Dorset Natural History and Archaeological Society*, XCIV (1972), pp.49-62. I owe this reference to Dr Colin Platt.
87. SA, LB, MT 616.
88. LB, Harleian MS, 6690.
89. SA, LB, box 417, account of Richard Pauntley; ibid, account of William Moille, bailiff of the Lord Edmund, Earl of March.
90. See pp.49-53.
91. See pp.53.
92. See p.62.
93. Faraday, 1991, pp.20-21.
94. Train, 1999, pp.10-11.

Chapter 6
1. Unless otherwise stated, all references are given in the chapter referred to.
2. See pp.28-30.
3. See p.27.
4. Ibid.
5. See pp.33-35, 49-53.
6. See pp.51-52.
7. See pp.17-18.
8. See pp.35-37.
9. See pp.35-37.
10. See p.35.
11. See p.38.
12. See pp.57-59.
13. See p.12.
14. Lloyd, D.W., *The Making of English Towns. 2000 years of evolution* (London, 1984), p.72.
15. See p.42.
16. See p.39.
17. See p.40.
18. Ibid.
19. See pp.41-42.
20. See p.65.
21. See pp.59-62.
22. See pp.67-69.
23. See pp.69-71.
24. See pp.43-44.
25. See p.44.
26. See p.25-26, 43.
27. See pp.56-57.
28. *Victoria County History, Shropshire*, II (1973), pp.95-96, 102-104.
29. See pp.71-74.
30. Hill, F., *A Short History of Lincoln* (Lincoln, 1979), pp.34-35; Hoskins, W.G., *Devon* (Newton Abbot, 1972 ed.), pp.504-07.
31. Bodleian Library Map Reproductions I: *The Map of Great Britain circa A.D.1360 known as The Gough Map* (Oxford, 1958).
32. See p.69-71.

Index